THIS BOOK BELONGS TO

WE ARE PHOTOGIRLS
DIY FASHION SHOOT BOOK

we are \\\ \\\
PHOTOGIRLS

Laurence King Publishing

LAURENCE KING

Published in 2014 by
Laurence King Publishing Ltd
361-373 City Road
London EC1V 1LR
United Kingdom
Tel: +44 20 7841 6900
Fax: +44 20 7841 6910
e-mail: enquiries@laurenceking.com
www.laurenceking.com

This book was produced by Laurence King
Publishing Ltd, London

Emily Stein and Celia Willis have asserted
their right under the Copyright, Designs,
and Patents Act 1988, to be identified as the
Authors of this Work.

A catalogue record for this book is available
from the British Library.
ISBN: 978-1-78067-299-1

Design: Eleanor Ridsdale
Illustrations: Rose Stallard
Senior editor: Peter Jones

Printed in China

Photograph on p.2 *Circus!* by Lucy Kenny

CONTENTS

HELLO FROM WE ARE PHOTOGIRLS

Welcome to our world, where fashion, style and beauty explode from each and every one of us. Embrace this book and before you know it you'll be spending your days running around the streets in extravagant outfits, hunting for bizarre fashion shoot locations, backcombing hair 'til it stands on end and photographing long into the night.

Absorb our secrets of how to run a successful fashion shoot and discover everything you need to know to become the best stylist, photographer, make-up artist, hair designer, art director and We Are Photogirls model.

Roam through the pages of this book, let your imagination run wild and create things that you never thought possible. Congratulations, you are now officially a Photogirl!

HOW TO USE THIS BOOK

- To get clued up, head straight into the Fashion Shoot Basics section. Everything you need to know to get started is here.

- The fashion shoots in this book are a mixture of ones you can tackle alone, with a friend or a whole bunch of you. Go solo or join forces, it's up to you.

- You don't have to buy anything to make our fashion shoots happen. Find, borrow or make do — the results might be even more interesting.

- You are more than capable of doing everything in this book.

- There are no rules that you have to stick to, only (hopefully) helpful suggestions.

- **Boys!** You can love this book too.

MANIFESTO

FALL IN LOVE WITH CREATING FASHION-SHOOTS • FIND INSPIRATION ALL AROUND YOU • CELEBRATE EVERYONE'S UNIQUE STYLE & BEAUTY • SCRIBBLE DOWN EVEN THE SMALLEST OF IDEAS • MAKE SCRAPBOOKS • WEAR WHAT YOU WANT • EXPLORE UNDISCOVERED SHOOT LOCATIONS • TAKE PICTURES TAKE PICTURES TAKE PICTURES • DON'T COMPARE YOURSELF TO OTHERS • IF AN IDEA DOESN'T WORK, KEEP GOING • DON'T OVER-THINK, CREATE • GIVE THE FASHION WORLD A RUN FOR ITS MONEY

OH! AND, DON'T EVER FORGET... THE MODELS AND CELEBRITIES THAT FILL MAGAZINE PAGES AREN'T ACTUALLY 'PERFECT', THEY ARE JUST PERFECTLY RETOUCHED! PLEASE REPEAT, SHARE AND REMEMBER.

WE ARE PHOTOGIRLS

Girls On Bikes
by Elaine Constantine

Fashion Shoot Basics

HOW TO RUN YOUR FASHION SHOOTS

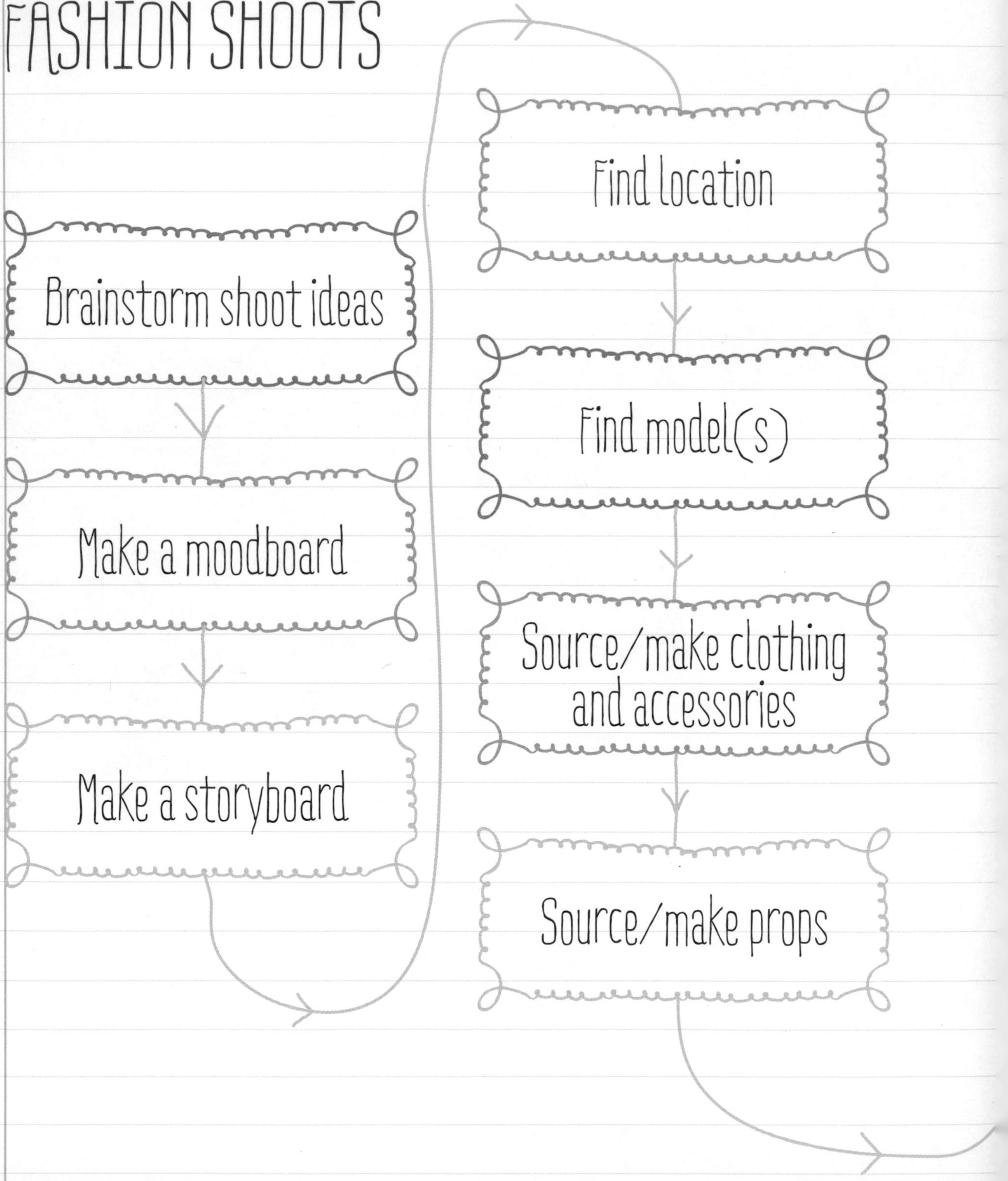

Brainstorm shoot ideas

↓

Make a moodboard

↓

Make a storyboard

Find location

↓

Find model(s)

↓

Source/make clothing and accessories

↓

Source/make props

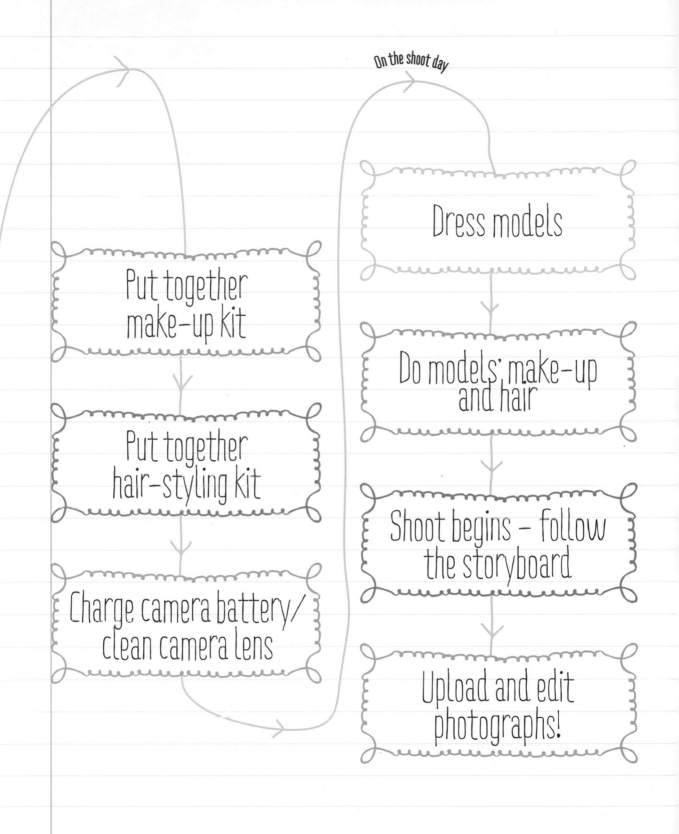

On the shoot day

Put together make-up kit

Put together hair-styling kit

Charge camera battery/ clean camera lens

Dress models

Do models' make-up and hair

Shoot begins – follow the storyboard

Upload and edit photographs!

THE ART OF TAKING BEAUTIFUL PHOTOGRAPHS

Open your eyes

Close your eyes and open them again very slowly. Now imagine that you are seeing everything for the first time. Look around you with fresh eyes. Notice the beauty in the colours, the people, the patterns and the shapes all around you. Everything has a special beauty, you just need to see it.

You don't need to be a tech geek to get to know your camera

If you want be in control of how your photographs turn out, you need to get to know your camera. If you're not a natural tech geek don't despair, you only need to learn a few basics to get going. If manuals bore you to tears, test things out for yourself. Try out different settings on your camera. Play around with shutter speeds, depth of field and exposure and see what happens. Watch online tutorials to get a hands-on approach to knowing your camera.

It's all about composition

When you are shooting, play around with where your model is placed within your frame. Remember, the model(s) don't have to be placed smack-bang in the centre of your frame, they can be positioned to the left, the right, the bottom, the top or partly cut out of the picture. When you think you've tried out all possible options, think of some more.

Take your camera everywhere

We can't stress this point enough. Take a camera with you everywhere you go as you never ever know when you are going to run into inspiration for your next fashion shoot. You might find a great location, a prop or an interesting hairstyle but if you don't have a camera you'll miss it!

Get candid

Keep an eye out when your model is relaxing in between shots. She/he may be stretching her/his arms, adjusting her/his shoe, talking to someone off-set or even yawning. Shoot her/him looking natural. These unexpected shots can sometimes be the best.

Let there be light

Create all kinds of atmospheres in your photographs by playing with light and use the weather to your advantage.

Sunny days – Early in the morning and late in the afternoon the light is soft, warm and romantic.

Bright midday sunlight can be tricky as it is very bright and casts harsh shadows on your model's face and body. If you want to shoot in these conditions, use your flash to eliminate shadows.

Cloudy days – Clouds diffuse the light, making it neutral and easy to photograph in. Another bonus of shooting on a cloudy day is that you don't have to watch out for shadows.

Stormy days – Stormy days are dark and moody, so if you choose to shoot on such a day, your photographs will look dark and moody too. Perfect if you want a dramatic feel to your photographs. Just watch out for drops of rain!

Move your feet

When photographing, the main thing to remember is to use your feet and move about while shooting. Shoot sideways, shoot front-on, kneel down, lie on the floor, stand on your tiptoes. Even jump on a ladder and shoot downwards. This is the only way to get unusual angles that will add interest to your photographs.

Make mistakes

Making mistakes is important. It's how we learn what works and what doesn't. OK, worst-case scenario: you've spent hours planning and photographing a shoot and you're not happy with the results. Annoying. Well, think about why it didn't work and pick apart what went wrong. You can then avoid these mistakes next time. We have all been in this situation before, the main thing is that you don't give up!

Practice makes perfect

It's a saying which we have all heard a million times before but it is true. The more fashion you photograph, the better a photographer you will become. If you want to become brilliant, keep shooting.

HOW TO MAKE A MOODBOARD

What is a moodboard?

An essential step in the preparation of any fashion shoot, moodboards are the best way to formulate your ideas, pin down your concept and communicate it to the rest of a fashion shoot team.

A moodboard is a chaotic collage of exciting items such as photographs, found images, colour samples and locations. Your moodboards should bustle with energy and leave everyone who sees them desperate to turn your vision into a reality.

The key thing to remember is that a moodboard is rough, ready and ever-changing, so you don't need to be precious about putting it together. You can either make them by (hand-) sticking images to card, paper, a wall or pinboard. Alternatively, put them together on a computer and then print them out.

Helpful items
- A large piece of paper/card, a pin board/wall space to pin onto •
Sticking material e.g. Blu- tack or masking tape • Millions of torn-out and found images • Scissors
- Or... just a computer

Step by step

1 If you are making your moodboards by hand, you need a large piece of paper or card to start with. Or use a pinboard or a wall as your background.

2 Gather together images that relate to your ideas for your shoot. Look online and print things out, rip pages from magazines and newspapers, grab postcards and flyers or photocopy from books. Find images that are of objects, props or locations that are similar to ones you would like to find and use in your shoot. Think abstractly too. You might find yourself tearing out a picture of an old Chinese vase because the pattern on it evokes the same old world oriental feeling that you want in your shoot.

3 Look out for pictures just for their colour or texture, as this will help you to communicate the general colour scheme of the shoot – crucial information for the stylist and make-up artist. A good trick is to go to any DIY shop and help yourself to the paint colour swatchcards . You can then have your own reference library in every colour of the rainbow.

4 When you are happy with your collection, stick or pin them to the card/paper/pinboard or wall. First, select the image that you think best sums up the shoot theme. Position it centrally, then layer and add the other images around it. Don't overthink – just add images ad hoc.

5 Keep playing around and have some fun until you are happy with what you have. Enjoy looking at how your shoot ideas are taking shape!

6 Show your moodboard to the rest of your fashion shoot team and get chatting about it.

P.S For a different way of working try out sites like Pinterest. This is an online site where you create an account to make pinboards. You can search the internet for images and then add them directly to your board; other people (including your fashion shoot team) can then go online to see what you have done.

HOW TO MAKE A STORYBOARD

Fashion shoots are made up of a series of photographs that tell a story. Each photograph tells a different part of that story. The details change within each picture, e.g. the model's clothing, facial expression or the props.

What is a storyboard?

Storyboards are sketches in which you plan out the photographs you want to take on your fashion shoots. A storyboard is the next thing to make once you have finished your moodboards. They don't have to be beautifully drawn: loose scribbles, stick men and little notes are what they are all about. Their sole purpose is to remind you when you are on your shoot of exactly how you want to set up each shot, so ponder over every last tiny detail.

Storyboards are crucial. Planning in advance gives you time to focus on exactly what you want in your photographs. Making it up as you go along on the day won't get you the best results as you will be distracted by a million and one other things. Not only are storyboards a great way of reminding you of what you want to capture; they are also the best way of communicating your ideas to the rest of your team!

Helpful Items
- Plain white paper -
Coloured pencils or felt-tips

Step by step

1 Decide how many shots you want to take. The amount is totally up to you, but be realistic with the time you will have on the shoot day. It's better to spend your shoot getting three perfect shots than rushing through ten.

2 Either use one small piece of paper per shot, or divide up one large piece into equal-sized boxes and plan out your whole shoot on one page.

3 Shot-by-shot, draw out what you want to see in each photograph. .

Take these things into consideration for each shot:

- Is it a close-up, medium or wide shot?
- How will the model(s) be posing? e.g. leaning, jumping or sitting?
- Where will the model(s) be positioned within the frame?
- What is your model's character? Are they serious, fun or thoughtful?
- If there is more than one model, how will they interact with each other and with the camera?
- What props or objects do you want to use?
- What is your location or backdrop?

Once you have made your storyboards and you think they are clear and precise, show them to the rest of the fashion shoot team.

Look how in *Wonderland — Afternoon Nap* Yeondoo Jung has playfully turned this kid's drawing into a striking image.

DON'T FORGET to keep your storyboards on you at all times during the shoot day. Follow them closely to get each shot perfect!

THE BRILLIANCE OF BACKDROPS

What is a backdrop?

In the simplest terms, a backdrop is a large piece of fabric or paper that you put up and use as a background for the model to stand in front of in a fashion shoot. What's great about a backdrop is that you can put it up anywhere and instantly transform any space into a professional photography studio. If you want the main focus of the shoot to be the models, the styling and the composition, backdrops are the way to go.

Professional backdrops are very expensive but luckily you don't need to splash out on these. You can easily make your own and no one will spot the difference. All you need to do is get hold of some good materials. You can make backdrops out of fabric, paper, card or wallpaper – each one has a time and place to be used, and all you need to do is to hang them up or stick them to a wall.

Photographer Louise
Dahl-Wolfe taken by
Robert Doisneau

Fabric

You can buy a huge array of fabrics from shops, but if you want to save your money use old bedsheets or curtains. Great for when you are shooting full-body shots and need a big backdrop.

Card

Using a large piece of card is a good option for photographing head-and-shoulder shots, or props, accessories and clothing that you have made. Card is easy to get hold of, inexpensive and comes in a multitude of colours. What's also great about card is that it doesn't crease like fabric.

P.S. Keep an eye out in art shops for huge rolls of white drawing paper. You can cover large areas with them and they are great value for money.

Wallpaper

Wallpaper is a great option if you are looking for a patterned background. It doesn't crease and if you buy a whole roll of it, it can cover a large surface for full-body shots. In lots of DIY shops you can help yourself to free samples to take home, so save your pennies and grab these freebies.

Miscellaneous finds

As long as you can pin it or stick to a wall, you can use any type of paper or fabric to make backdrops. Don't overlook magazines, newspapers, postcards, posters or wrapping paper. If you're good with a brush and paints, or a needle and thread you can patchwork or paint your own original backdrops.

Really important tips to remember

When you are working with backdrops, there are a few important things to remember. You desperately want to avoid your backdrop looking shoddy, or it will let your whole shoot down!

- Make sure that your backdrop is as crease-free as possible. If it's fabric, iron it before a shoot and always fold it away neatly after using it. If it's paper or card, roll it carefully before storing it.

- Make sure that the backdrop is long enough and wide enough to fill your frame. It may need to run down onto the floor so that the model can stand on it. If you are shooting full body you may need to stitch, tape or pin two pieces of your chosen backdrop material together to create extra width.

- You don't want to accidentally photograph any of the sides, top or bottom of your backdrop. Avoid this by standing your models in the middle of the backdrop.

IMPORTANT!!!! Only use thick masking tape or electrical tape to stick your backdrop to the wall — any other types of tape may rip off paintwork when you take the backdrop down.

Beachobatics by George Caddy

The Many Lives of a Photogirl

BE A WE ARE PHOTOGIRLS MODEL

Becoming a We Are Photogirls model is a very different thing to becoming a conventional model. You see, a conventional model needs to be of a certain height and have specific body measurements. But a We Are Photogirls model just needs to be herself. No matter what your shape, size or height you can be the ultimate We Are Photogirls model.

On hearing this, you might think 'but people look better in photographs if they are really tall and skinny'. The reality is, we only think this because that is the current trend in adverts, celebrity culture and magazines. If you look back through the ages, you'll see that models' body shapes have constantly changed. In the 1950s models were voluptuous and curvy, whereas the original 1980s supermodels were athletic, Amazonian women. So, let's get over the idea that our body shape determines whether or not we can be a great model. Instead, let's focus on the most important factor in modelling – confidence in front of the camera.

So how do I do it?

Being a We Are Photogirls model is all about letting go and having fun. Be confident. Enjoy your own beauty. The main thing to master is how to relax in front of the camera. Think of the camera as your friend not your enemy. If you don't feel 100 per cent sure about your looks and worry that you don't have what it takes to model in a fashion shoot, you are very wrong. You can be a great model. In a fashion shoot the photographer takes hundreds of photographs. Yes, some WILL be unflattering but some WILL be stunning, and these are the only ones that you will keep. Ignore the photographs that you don't like and concentrate on the ones that you do. Even professional models whom we think are flawless have their own insecurities and certainly have unflattering photographs taken of them. We just never see any of these. We only see the best ones and these have also been retouched; a 'magical' process where the normality of cellulite, spots, bags and broken veins vanishes.

BEFORE THE SHOOT

Get a good night's sleep before the big shoot day. Wake up fresh as a daisy and ready to look your best.

Drink plenty of water to hydrate your skin and to give you lots of energy.

Brush your hair so it's clean and knot-free for the hair stylist. No one wants to work with greasy, tangled locks!

Get together some photographs that give you inspiration for poses you might want to try out.

Make sure that your face is clean and make-up free, so it's ready for the make-up artist.

DURING THE SHOOT

Enjoy the experience. When you are older, you will be really pleased to have these photographs of your youth.

Be spontaneous, try out lots of different poses and expressions. Sometimes you may feel like a bit of an idiot but the weirdest compositions can create the greatest pictures.

Don't try and pose like you think a model ought to pose. Bring your own character and personality into the photographs; this will bring them to life.

Don't just stand still in one spot. Move around and interact with your location.

If you don't know what to do, grab hold of some props. It can be really helpful to have something to hold and mess around with.

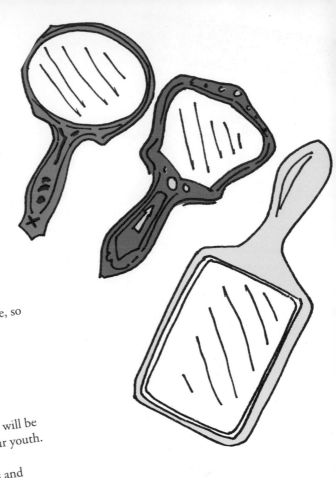

Everyone Is Beautiful

It is easy to see what is beautiful about other people, but sometimes hard to see what is beautiful about ourselves. This is exactly why Everyone Is Beautiful can only happen with the help of a valued and trusted friend. Working on each other, your task is to bring out what makes each other beautiful, and to celebrate your discoveries in a fashion portrait. Everyone has something to celebrate so find something original in your friend's appearance, or travel deeper and find it in their soul. Do they have sun-kissed freckles? Are they a die-hard music fan? Do they have seriously curly hair? Or are they obsessed with the colour black?

Kim, 15, Tampa, Florida
by Danielle Levitt

Untitled from the *Qajar* series,
1998 by Shadi Ghadirian

Step by step

1 Get together and brainstorm ideas. Sit opposite each other and write down everything you think is amazing about the other person! List personality traits, appearance, style, hobbies and interests.

2 You are going to style and photograph your friend's portrait and vice versa so, next, go through your list and decide what element about them you will focus on as the theme for their fashion shoot.

3 How will you dress them? Will they wear make-up? How will you style their hair? All these choices will make a big difference to the portrait you make.

4 Next, think through possible locations and props for their shoot. These are powerful ways to add layers of information about your friend.

The shoot

- Draw out storyboards so that you know exactly what shots you want to get.

- Getting a great portrait isn't easy! Photographers have to be patient in finding *that* moment where the camera really captures someone's essence. Keep going until you feel you have truly captured your friend's personality on camera. Don't be afraid to ask them to try out different poses or expressions Sometimes it's about using your intuition to get what you want.

- Try shooting against a white backdrop as well as whatever location you have chosen. A plain backdrop can change the whole feel of a fashion portrait and can really help to make a personality stand out.

Pearls of wisdom

- Personal items are an excellent way to express something about your friend, so get prop hunting through their precious possessions.

- If you are using a friend's hobby as your theme, think about interesting ways to photograph it, e.g. if they are a keen trampolinist you could photograph them flying through the air in a beautiful evening dress.

BE A MAKE-UP ARTIST

A make-up artist is just like a painter: they both create wonders using only a brush and a palette of colours. The major difference is that a make-up artist's paints come in the form of make-up pigments, and her canvas is the human face and body. Make-up artists learn to be extremely neat and obsessively precise. Their canvas is only small so they have to get everything absolutely spot-on or all their hard work could turn into an uncontrollable mess! Noticing the hidden beauty in everyone, a make-up artist works skilfully to bring this to the surface for all to see

A make-up artist doesn't just follow what's fashionable now, she draws from the past as well as shaping the future. A sucker for patterns, shapes and colours, she sees everything through a looking glass. From the vibrant tones of exotic flowers to the metallic shades of a junkyard, the colours surrounding her inform her ideas and designs. One day she may be working on a chic and glamorous burlesque shoot, the next she could be plastering a gaggle of models head to toe in neon paint. One day is never the same as the next and there is never a dull moment!

What do they do?

A make-up artist designs the make-up looks for a fashion shoot, working with the rest of the fashion photography team to gain an understanding of the mood and feel of the shoot. She'll work closely with the stylist and hair stylist. She then plans the make-up looks that will complement the styling and hair designs. These looks can range from unique patterns designed by the make-up artist to classic looks taken from a specific era. She must work against the ticking clock to work her magic and will also be on hand during the shoot to apply any touch-ups.

Be as neat and precise as you can.

Think about colours and patterns and how they complement each other. Don't believe 'facts' such as 'never put red next to pink or blue with black'...mixing things up is the way to go!

Tips to help you on your way

Always draw out your designs on paper before you start working on the face.

Make-up doesn't show up as strongly in a photograph as it does when we look at it in reality. Try adding a little extra to make sure it stands out in the photographs.

Always test make-up on your model's skin to check that they are not allergic to it.

SO HOW DO I DO IT?

Before the shoot

1. Consider the theme and atmosphere of the shoot you are working on, moodboard ideas. Think about colour schemes as well as researching on the internet, looking in books and in magazines to find out how specific looks are achieved.

2. Draw out each design for each model to see which colours and ideas work best. If you're planning on changing make-up looks for different shots, make sure you keep your designs in order.

3. If you have designed something quite complicated, test it out before the big shoot day. If you can't find anyone to practise on, sit in front of a mirror and work on yourself.

4. Make sure that you have gathered all the equipment and make-up you need! Remember, it's not essential to have shop-bought make-up brushes as these can be expensive. You can use paintbrushes or improvise or use everyday items found around the house. Look for ones with a thin, blunt edge – cotton buds or the bottom end of a spoon work well. Think outside the box and test out whatever you can find.

On the shoot

1. Make sure the model is dressed before you start working on the make-up; this way nothing gets smudged.

2. Begin working on the model(s), taking your time to make sure you get everything just right.

3. When the photographer begins shooting check the first few images to see that the make-up looks good, if not ,jump in and make speedy corrections!

4. Keep your kit on you at all times and be aware of the model as the make-up will need touching up. If possible do this is in between shots so that you don't disturb the flow of things on the shoot.

A make-up artist's toolkit

Mascara
Liquid eyeliner
Various lipstick shades
Various lipliner shades
Eye-shadow palettes
Fake eyelashes
Various nail varnish shades
Stick-on gems
Blushers
Talcum powder
Cotton buds
Baby wipes/warm soapy water
Eyelash curlers
Bronzers
Various foundation shades
Face paints

TRIBE

Tribal make-up just never seems to go out of style. Starting out life with indigenous tribes living in remote parts of the world, these days it can be seen reinventing itself in fashion magazines, music videos, high street trends and on the fast-paced catwalk of any international fashion week.

Take tribal make-up to the next level. Be as traditional or as postmodern as you dare. Imagine brave, bright and colourful designs and let them roam all over the face, hands, arms, legs, knees and feet. The bolder, the better. Colour outside the lines.

Helpful items
• Face paints • Brushes • Sponges • Coloured pencils/ felt-tips and paper

The shoot

- Depending on whether your make-up design covers the whole body or just the face, decide how close you are going to photograph your model(s). If you are shooting with space around them, make sure you choose a background suited to your make-up. Notice how the simple black background in the inspiration photo makes the primary coloured make-up really stand out.

- Before shooting, make sure your make-up is really neat! Even if you want a wild look, there is a fine line between it looking spontaneous and a total mess.

Step by step

1 Time to design. Come up with ideas and draw them out. Take inspiration from an existing, tribal make-up 'look' or create your own.

2 The three main design elements to concentrate on are colour, pattern and repetition. Will you clash colours or use complementary ones? Will you work out a system of repeating patterns, such as zigzags followed by stripes, zigzags followed by stripes and so on...

3 Cover the face/body in a base colour and then add your designs on top. To do this, get a sponge and spread a thin layer of facepaint onto the skin with a stroking motion. Even out any inconsistencies in the face paint by adding more, or by thinning heavy areas. Pat the skin with the sponge to get a smooth, all-over look. If you want to create a thick base, apply several coats and let each one dry before you add the next.

4 Now get to work on the patterns, following your designs carefully. If you don't have the exact make-up or tools that you need, be inventive. Experiment with cutting up old sponges and rags to get the application you want, and remember, normal paintbrushes can make great make-up brushes.

Bridget by Olaf Breuning

P.S. Test face paint on your model's skin to check that they are not allergic to it.

WE ♥ PAT McGRATH

Pat McGrath is one of the most incredible make-up artists of our time and her revolutionary work leaves us speechless. Pat is a lesson to us all – she didn't have any formal training in make-up design but didn't let that stand in her way. She perfected her designs and rose to fame with her inventive work which featured in British style magazines such as *The Face*, *ID* and *Dazed and Confused*.

Her rule-breaking style is truly one of a kind: she prefers to use her fingertips rather than brushes, she experiments with her own make-up made from powder paints, and she has even created 3D 'off the face' make-up made from plastic and latex. What a legend…

A model presents a creation designed by John Galliano, 20 January 2003 in Paris for Christian Dior Spring/Summer 2003 Haute Couture collection

A model on the runway at the Christian Dior Spring/Summer 2008 collection fashion show

Helpful items
- Colourful make-up •
Stickers • Anything you can
cut into shapes – be it card,
plastic or foam • Vaseline

The shoot

- To get the most flattering close-up shots of your model's face and make-up design use your camera's zoom to focus on the face – this flattens and softens the model's features.

- Play around with coloured filters on this shoot – they will add an overall colour caste to your photographs. You can buy these cheaply online or at a camera shop. Alternatively, find a see-through, coloured plastic stationery folder and shoot through it.

Step by step

1 Forget the natural look, think of ideas that would leave Pat McGrath gasping in wonder! Make her proud, ignore traditional make-up conventions. Grab paper and pens and start sketching wild and imaginative make-up designs. It's a good idea to draw out a basic face shape and then fill it with your designs.

2 Think 3-D! Include cut-out shapes, letters and stickers to emulate Pat McGrath's style. When it comes to sticking these to the face, use Vaseline as your glue. If your shapes are quite heavy you may have to use some eyelash glue to get the extra hold.

3 Before you start work on the face, lay out everything that you will be using and test out products that aren't make-up on an area of the model's skin, like her arm – you don't want to cause an allergic reaction!

4 Start creating your design on the face. Take your time, follow your drawings and make sure that you apply your make-up and shapes as neatly as possible.

5 Think of a hairstyle that will work with your make-up look. This can be as simple or as complicated as you like, from scraping the entire hair back into a tight, sophisticated bun, or crimping the hair to create crazy volume.

TEARS OF A CLOWN

Love them or hate them, for some unknown reason clowns bring out a strong reaction in all of us. Their make-up is unmistakable, charismatic and impossible to forget. In the old-school world of clowning, every single clown invents their very own trademark make-up design; and no other clown would ever dare to wear it.

In your mind wander through stripey big-top tents filled with unicycles, honking horns, bad pranks and multi-coloured wigs. Now grab your make-up brushes and bring your own clown to life.

Step by step

1 First, create the personality for your clown. Yours could be a sweet-natured candy-coloured clown or a dark, twisted sinister clown. Let the clown's personality influence your make-up ideas and start sketching.

2 Recruit a model, or work on yourself. Start off by giving the face a quick wash to get rid of any make-up. For those with sensitive skin, put a thin layer of moisturiser on to protect it.

3 To begin with, you need to create a base for your designs to sit on. Use your sponge to spread a thin layer of facepaint onto the entire face and neck with a stroking motion. Even out any inconsistencies in the face paint by adding more, or by thinning heavy areas. To make sure you have a smooth look all over, pat the whole face and neck with the sponge. If you want to create a thick base, then apply several coats, letting each one dry out properly before you add the next.

4 Now it's time to add the colour and designs to the face. For larger parts of the design you can use a clean make-up sponge. If you want to add finer details, use a brush. After adding a colour, let it set before applying the next one – this will stop them from smudging into each other. If you only have one brush or sponge, make sure you clean it thoroughly between colours.

5 When you have completed the make-up design, don't forget to style your clown's hair. You could slick the hair back with colourful face paints, or frizz it up and add a huge bow.

6 For a final touch make a traditional clown's hat. All you need for this is a large rectangular piece of card or stiff paper. Roll it into a cone with a point at the top, mark and then trim around the bottom to get a clean circle that can balance on the head. Decorate it as you please.

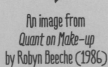

An image from
Quant on Make-up
by Robyn Beeche (1986)

- A few colourful face paints • A squidgy sponge • Some make-up/normal paintbrushes • Coloured crayons

The shoot

- Think about what background would best suit your make-up. Simple backgrounds can really help a make-up design to stand out in a photograph, but seeing a clown in an unusual location can make for a great fashion story.

- Don't forget that your clown should have a personality behind the make-up. Storyboard ideas for how you want your clown to interact with the camera.

Queen Bee Marie

France's iconic but ill-fated queen, Marie Antoinette, has always been known for her trademark make-up. In the eighteenth century it was very hip to be extremely pale and Marie really got it right with her porcelain 'living doll' look. Mastering this old-fashioned trend is actually pretty simple; you just need to follow the steps below.

Step by step

1 Add a pale foundation to the face, preferably a few shades lighter than your skin tone. This will create that doll-like flawless finish.

2 Tip some talcum powder into a bowl then dust the face, neck, chest and lips with a blusher brush or make-up sponge.

3 Add dark brown or black eye-shadow to the eyebrows. You need to make the eyebrows a few shades darker than they naturally are so that they stand out.

4 Apply blusher in dramatic circles to the centre of the cheeks.

5 Add a light-coloured, pearly eye-shadow to the eyelids, sweeping right up to the eyebrows.

6 Apply fake eyelashes or outrageous amounts of mascara.

7 Lastly, shape the lips into a rosebud. To do this, draw a heart shape with a red lip pencil in the centre of the lips, then fill it in with red lipstick. Make sure the rest of the lips outside the rosebud shape are covered in talcum powder too so that they completely disappear into the rest of the face.

8 Now you have transported your model back in time don't forget that it is crucial to match the era of your hairstyle to the era of your make up. Think volume & ringlets galore!

Helpful items

• Fake eyelashes or bucketfuls of black mascara • Pale foundation or a light moisturiser • Eye-shadows and lipsticks • Talcum powder • Blusher (or you can use a pink or red eye-shadow) • Lip pencils to match your lipstick shades

The shoot

- Remember you want the main focus of your photographs to be your make-up design. Shoot no wider than head and shoulders or else your make-up masterpiece will get lost in the frame.

- You will need a good amount of light for the camera to pick up the fine details of your pale make-up.

Queen Marie Antoinette (1755–93) by Jean-Etienne Liotard (1702–89)

BE A
HAIR STYLIST

The first thing you'll notice about a hair stylist is that she'll be sporting an incredible hair-do. She spends hours poring over fashion magazines, keeping up to date with the latest hair trends, working out how she will put her own magical twist on them. She'll also experiment with adapting traditional hair styles and designing her own brand-new, never-before-seen creations. Her cupboards are stuffed with bags bulging with specialist hair tools waiting to be whipped out for the next fashion shoot.

What do they do?

A hair stylist starts out by looking at the moodboards and storyboards for a shoot, then discusses the desired look(s) with the rest of the fashion photography team. Working within the theme of the shoot, she'll come up with ideas for the hair style(s). The shoot might call for a period style, a mix of traditional and contemporary, or a one-off original style. She'll work with the stylist and make-up artist to ensure her ideas tie in with the rest of the model's look.

On the day of the shoot she'll style the models' hair. While the shoot is going on she'll be alert and on-hand to rearrange and touch up any hair that might fall out of place.

Tips to help you on your way

Gather inspiration. Follow the latest hairstyles through blogs and magazines, as well as collecting inspiring hair-dos from the past. Start making scrapbooks of all the hair styles that excite you.

Practice makes perfect. Everyone loves having their hair done, so ask friends and family if you can experiment on them. Offer to do people's hair for special occasions and nights out. You'll soon find your services are in high demand.

Use sites like YouTube to your advantage. There are literally thousands of video tutorials that show step-by-step instructions of how to create different hairstyles. Watching 'live' is an easy way to learn a technique.

Use dry shampoo to add texture to your model's hair – this will make it much easier to style.

SO HOW DO I DO IT?

Before the shoot

1 Look at the moodboards and storyboards and come up with ideas for the hairstyles. Discussing your ideas with the team, you'll gauge how traditional or how unconventional they want the hairstyles to be. If there is more than one hairstyle per model, work out how you will move from one style to the next.

2 Practice the hairstyles you are going to create so that you are 100 per cent confident on the day.

3 Make a list of the models' names and the different hairstyles needed for each. This will help you stay on top of things if it gets busy and frantic on the shoot.

4 Prepare your kit. Go through your list and make sure you have all the tools and products that you are going to need.

On the shoot

1 Get your models ready. You'll be working to a deadline so stay calm and work methodically. You'll need to pay attention to detail to make sure that there isn't a single hair out of place.

2 Keep an eye on any models who are being photographed to ensure that their hair is picture-perfect.

3 Don't be afraid to stop your photographer and jump in and out of the set to tweak hair as needed.

A hair stylist's toolkit

Combs and brushes of all shapes and sizes

Bands, clips and clamps

Hairspray

Hair gel

Straighteners

Tongs

Crimpers

Hair extensions

Dry shampoo

Hair pins

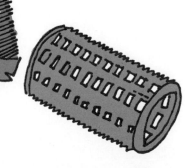

Le French Twist

Audrey Hepburn from the
1961 Blake Edwards film
Breakfast at Tiffany's

If there was ever a hairstyle that embodied elegance and sophistication it's le French twist. Worn with chic evening wear or casual daywear it works its glamorous magic, leaving you feeling like a modern-day Audrey Hepburn. Need to add a touch of golden age Hollywood to a fashion shoot? Look no further than the French twist hairstyle. If it's good enough for *Breakfast at Tiffany's*, it's good enough for us.

Step by step

1 Brush all the hair over to one side.

2 Use a few kirby grips to keep the hair in place. Push the kirby grips in at the nape of the neck.

3 With one hand, hold the hair out to the side. Place the thumb of your other hand in the middle of your model's head, then wrap the ponytail around your thumb.

4 Hold the twist in place with one hand while you take your thumb out.

5 Still holding the twist in place, use the hair pins to secure it. Be generous with the pins, use as many as you need to keep the twist in position (if you've never used hairpins before, you push them in, then round and back on themselves).

6 Once your French twist is held firm, hairspray the entire head for extra hold and your elegant French twist is complete.

Helpful items
- Hairbrush • Hairspray •
Kirby grips • Hairpins. NOT
the same as kirby grips!
(we've added a picture of
some to show you).

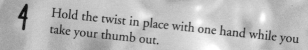

THE FISHTAIL PLAIT

The fishtail plait looks like a traditional plait but one that's had its insides pulled out! The style looks like something that could only be achieved by a pro hairstylist but actually it's surprisingly easy to do. You can style your fishtail plait to be elegantly neat or purposefully messy. You don't have to stop with a single plait either: once you've got the hang of what you're doing, you can start experimenting with multiple plaits and add unusual accessories to your creations. But before you go plait-crazy, you need to learn the basics.

Roses Are Red But My Sweater Is Pink by Sunshine Tucker

Helpful items

- A comb or brush
- A hairband

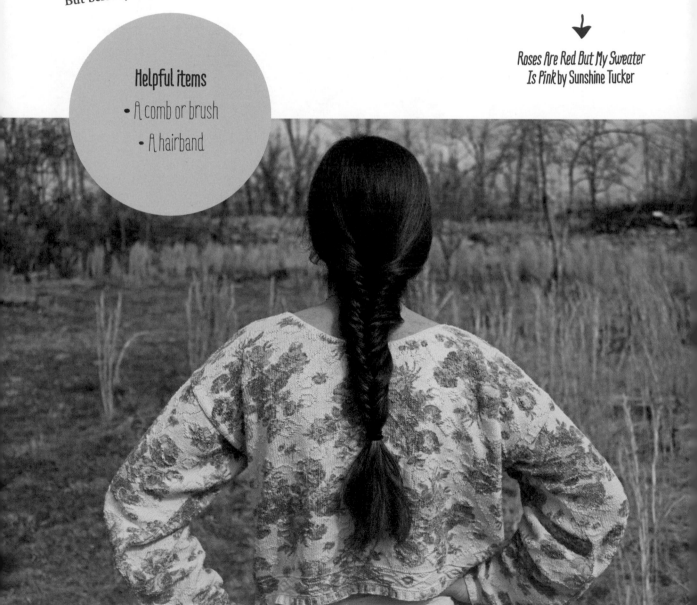

TIPS TO MAKING...

- A neat and tidy fishtail: use the same thickness for each strand that you plait your hairstyle with.

- A loose and messy fishtail: do exactly the opposite, use different amounts of hair in each strand. Then use your fingers to loosen the strands until your fishtail is as messy as you like.

Step by step

1 Make sure that the hair is clean, brushed and knot-free.

2 Now divide the hair into two parts straight down the middle of the scalp. Let's call these sections A and B. (It doesn't matter which is A and which is B.)

3 Next, take a strand of hair from the underneath of A side. Pull this strand outside the A side and over the top, crossing over and then joining the B side. Basically, the hair has looped over the A side and then joined the B side.

4 Now do exactly the same thing with the B side of the hair. Pull a strand out from the underneath of the B side, take it over the B side and leave it with the A side. Make the plait as loose or as tight as you want it to be, tighter is easier for beginners!

5 Repeat these steps until you reach the very bottom of the hair.

6 Phew! The hard part is over (and it wasn't that bad was it?). Now you can finish off your wonderful fishtail by tying it together with a hairband. If you want to give it a bit more personality, add clips, flowers, a colourful ribbon or hand-made accessories.

BUILD ME A BEEHIVE

Aim higher than the Eiffel Tower and the Empire State Building and build a towering beehive of your very own. Just an everyday hair-do for any fashion-conscious girl in the 1950s, the beehive has firmly stood the test of time (with a little help from its many celebrity friends). What's great is that it doesn't matter what length or thickness your hair is either. With a super-sized can of XXX-tra strong hairspray anyone's hair can be whipped into a superb beehive…

Step by step

1 Find a willing model and don't let her wash her hair! It's easier to create this look if the hair is a bit dirty. Let her hair down and spray her whole head lightly with hairspray.

2 Separate her hair into three sections – the top, the middle and the bottom. The middle and the bottom sections should be roughly the same amounts as each other, but the top section should only be a thin slice of her hair. This section will be used to cover up the nest you are about to make. Clip back the top and the bottom sections, as you only need the middle section to build the beehive.

3 Now backcombing begins. (Turn to the next page if you need help with how to backcomb.) Start backcombing the middle section from above the crown. The best way to get the most volume is by backcombing in small sections. Add hairspray to the roots to give the hair extra hold. Backcomb until her hair stands up on end!

4 When you are happy with your work, unclip the top section of hair and smooth it over your backcombing to create a flawless look for the beehive. Lightly hairspray it and use the kirby grips to hold it all together.

5 Well done. The hardest part is over. All that is left to do is to unclip the bottom section of the hair and brush it neatly.

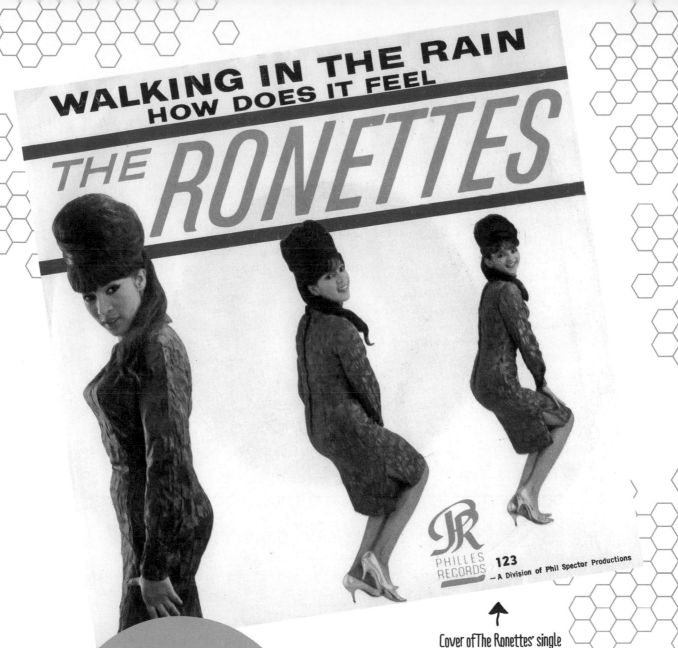

WALKING IN THE RAIN
HOW DOES IT FEEL

THE RONETTES

PHILLES RECORDS **123**
— A Division of Phil Spector Productions

Cover of The Ronettes' single
'Walking in the Rain'

Helpful items

- Cans of super-strong hairspray
- A fine-toothed comb
- A few kirby grips

The shoot

- Pay homage to the beehive's glory days and try your hand at a spot of 1950s styling. Tie a headscarf around the beehive in a front knot. Think powder puff skirts, polka dot shirts and kitten heels. When it comes to the make-up, treat your model to eyeliner flicks, bright red lipstick and beauty spots.

- Photographing your model from the side will show off the height and structure of your amazing beehive.

MY HAIR IS BIGGER THAN YOUR HAIR COMPETITION

My hair is bigger than your hair is more than a competition, it's a craze. Invite your friends over, armed with hairspray and brushes, set the stopwatch and head into a backcombing frenzy. Forget glossy, straight, silky smooth locks… instead embrace the frizzy, the wild and the enormous. Employ the ancient art of backcombing and see just how big you and your friends can get your hair to go!

PS Be really careful when you use hairspray. Getting it in the eyes or mouth is horrible! Before you spray someone tell them to hold their breath and to close their eyes.

The competition

Arrange a time and date for your 'comb-off'. Make sure you allow enough time not only for the competition, but for a photo shoot afterwards to capture the hairdos on camera. Set up a room in your house for the competition to take place in. Good ventilation is important. With a group of friends all busting out the hairspray you will need plenty of fresh air in the room! Set up competition stations with mirrors/hairspray/brushes/clips. You can create a 'mini salon' by bringing in chairs or putting towels on the floor for everyone to sit on. Work in pairs for the competition.

Before the competition can begin, it's up to you to explain how to backcomb. There are two different ways to do it. Encourage the competitors to try either, or combine both for added volume.

Downward backcombing

- Take a small section of hair (you may want to use clips or bands to hold the rest of the hair away if you need to).

- Hold the section of hair upwards towards the sky.

- Keeping a gentle but firm grip on the hair with one hand, take a brush or comb with the other hand and start brushing the hair in a downwards motion, towards the floor. Keep going until it looks like a knotted mass.

- Grab your hairspray and spray the section you have done to hold the volume. Now take another section and repeat. Keep going until you have a full head of backcombing done.

Upward backcombing

- Take a small section of hair (you may want to use clips or bands to hold the rest of the hair away if you need to).

- Hold the section of hair and gently pull it out sideways, away from the head at a slight angle.

- Keeping a gentle but firm grip on the hair with one hand, take a brush or comb with the other hand and start brushing the hair in an upwards motion, towards the sky. Keep going until it looks like a knotted mass.

- Grab your hairspray and spray the section you have done to hold the volume! Now take another section and repeat. Keep going until you have a full head of backcombing done.

READY, STEADY, GO!

Set an alarm clock for 15 minutes time, make a grab for your brushes and backcomb as fast as you can.

When the alarm starts ringing it's time for everyone to put down their brushes.

Judging can now commence. Who has created the biggest hairdo? Use a ruler to find out *exactly* whose is the biggest!

Members of The Jimi Hendrix
Experience doing their
hair, c. 1968

A quick post-shoot competition
- You've got fabulous hairdos, but before the shoot don't forget to add make-up. A bright shade of lipstick and a good coating of mascara should do it.
- Group shots of all the competitors together is a definite, as well as a portrait of the winning hairstyle!

BE A
STYLIST

A fashion stylist lives in a world of technicolour surrounded by clothing, jewellery and accessories. She is a collector and a bit of a hoarder and spends her time running around in search of bizarre pieces that will look fantastic in the right shoot. She isn't afraid to mix and match the latest trends with fashions from bygone eras and she loves to play with colour.

What do they do?

A fashion stylist's responsibilities on a shoot work like this. Firstly, she'll dream up and moodboard ideas for 'the look' of a shoot, then she'll source or make the outfits and accessories she has decided upon. On the day of the shoot she dresses the models meticulously and then keeps a careful, constant eye out for anything that may need adjusting.

In simple terms, anything and everything a model wears is down to the stylist.

SO HOW DO I DO IT?

Before the shoot

1 Considering the theme and the atmosphere of the shoot you are working on, moodboard your ideas. Think about colour schemes, textures, prints and fabrics. Your inspiration can come from anywhere. It may not even be from fashion, e.g. an old photograph of brightly coloured tropical birds may inspire you to use clothes with a similar colour scheme.

2 Source or make all the outfits you need for the shoot. When you have gathered them all together, label them clearly with the model's name and the shot that the clothing is for. e.g 'Marie, Shot 1. In field.' This will really save you time on the day.

A stylist's toolkit

Stylist's clamps

(you could use clamps available from any hardware shops)

Safety pins

Sharp scissors

A basic sewing kit

Travel iron

A selection of tapes and fabric glues for customizing

On the shoot

- Your job on the shoot is to be super-organized and on top of any clothing or accessory problems. When dressing the model, the clothing must fit them beautifully. Achieve this with stylist's clamps, pulling in the garments at the back or on the side of the model's body.

- When the shoot begins, watch the models closely to ensure that as they move in between shots the clothing is still hanging perfectly.

- Don't be afraid to stop your photographer and jump in and out of the set to re-adjust and rearrange. Making sure that everything is picture-perfect is a crucial part of your job.

Tips to help you on your way

Start a 'Stylist's Box'. Keep an eye out for one-of-a-kind pieces so that you can build up your own collection of items. As well as looking for clothing, it's a good idea to collect fabrics, belts, scarves and oddball accessories.

Don't follow the trends, create your own. Be unusual. How would you style clothes in ways that you wouldn't usually see? e.g. layer seven skirts on top of each other.

Make and customize. Creating your own unique accessories and customizing clothes is one of the joys of being a stylist. Try some ideas out and get making.

Stuck for where to get hold of new, cutting-edge clothes for shoots? Try to strike up friendships with independent clothing shops nearby. The idea is that you borrow their clothes and in return you give them copies of the photographs. Just remember to take really good care of their clothes or you may end up having to pay for them!

Scour for bargains. Part of the challenge of being a stylist is working within a budget, so buy as cheaply as you can. Hunt online on sites like eBay and spend your weekends rooting around jumble sales, village fairs and charity shops. If an item isn't quite right, but has the potential to be incredible, buy it and rejig it yourself.

Emulate a Style Icon

From the rebellious Lady Gaga to the glamorous Grace Kelly, you won't have to look far to find a style icon to emulate. We all adore different ones depending on our personal taste. Mexican artist Frida Kahlo is one of our own personal favourites. Not only did she have her own characteristic style and beauty, but she was also a revolutionary artist. Mixing folksy boho clothing with an avant-garde outlook, her trademarks were the way she wore her plaited hair, her unibrow, giant statement jewellery and big, floral Mexican dresses.

We love dressing like Frida for the day so it's time to ask yourself who would you like to dress as? Be it true eccentric Grace Jones or classic pin-up Marilyn Monroe, its time for you to take your pick.

Step by step

1 It's thinking time. Who are your favourite style icons and which one of these would you like to emulate in a shoot? Write a list of who you think are the best-dressed musicans, artists, actresses, and fashion personalities from the past to the present day. You could also emulate an icon during just a very specific stage of their career, e.g. David Bowie in the 1970s.

2 Research your icon. Take note of every tiny visual detail – their style, favoured colour schemes, regular hairstyles and make-up choices but also importantly their celebrity persona. Are they gentle, brooding, ditsy or outrageous? To emulate their style to perfection you will need to echo their personality in your fashion shoot. If you want to make things really easy, find a photograph of your style icon that you feel sums them up and replicate it detail for detail.

3 Gather together your wardrobe. Beg and borrow! Hunt high and low for pieces that you think will work. Get customizing if you need to.

4 Design your hair and make-up look, and if you are attempting anything complicated make sure to test it out before your shoot.

5 Find a helpful friend to photograph you, or, if your camera has a self-timer, use it. If you don't fancy modelling, then cast a friend as a model and photograph the shoot yourself.

6 Location. Where will you shoot your photographs? Where has your style icon been photographed in the past? Can you find a similar type of location near you? If not, go for a simple background which will really help your styling to stand out.

7 How will you pose in the photographs? Pore over images of your icon and practice mimicking their characteristic body language and facial expressions.

Frida on a White Bench by Nickolas Muray

The shoot

- If you are using a photographer, be sure to make storyboards for them otherwise they won't know what you want them to shoot. Although you will probably want to see every shot just as soon as they have taken it, it's better not to put them off their stride. Let them shoot loads of shots in a row before stopping to review those you have got so far.

- To help really capture the style and personality of your chosen icon, imagine that you really *are* them, and stay in character the whole time that you are being photographed.

- Set up shots that look candid and unposed. Stay in character, but ignore the camera and see if your photographer can capture some documentary-style shots. Try laughing at something off camera, tying your shoelaces or talking to achieve that 'natural' look.

Helpful items
- Pictures/posters/postcards of your style icon

SEEING DOUBLE

Conjure up a pair of matching twins, put your styling skills on overdrive and breathe life into them. Mirror and mimic every single part of their being, from their clothes and make-up to their body language and facial expressions. Style your way into a hypnotic world of repetition, duplication and imitation and don't stop until you are genuinely confused as to who is who.

Swimsuit Girls of Old Japan

• Identical clothes • Identical shoes • Identical hats • Identical bags • Identical hairstyles • Identical grins • Identical poses • Identical everything

Before the shoot

1 Find two friends to transform into twins. If you're looking for an easy ride, pick models with similar hair and eye colour, or make it quirkier and choose models who couldn't look more different from each other.

2 Work out your styling. How many items can you rustle up that are exactly the same? To give you more choice, borrow from friends' wardrobes. Either use the same types of clothing e.g. pyjamas, school uniforms, swimsuits, or hunt for clothing of the same colour or that have matching patterns. And don't forget to look for matching accessories and objects to use as props.

3 If you can't find duplicates of anything that you love, make your own outfits. Ditto for props and accessories.

4 Hair and make-up time! Complement your styling by mimicking its colour schemes and patterns in the make-up you use. Be sure to give your twins matching hairstyles too.

Helpful items
• Any items of clothing, accessories and props that you can get more than one of
• A 'pair' of friends

5 Get location hunting. Look for repeated patterns in your surroundings e.g. a tiled floor or a row of identical houses. Alternatively, go for a repeat pattern in a backdrop, such as polka dots or striped fabric.

6 Storyboard out your shots and prepare the twins for the shoot!

The shoot

• Be a control freak! For the shoot to really work, the models must mimic and mirror each other completely, down to the tiniest, microscopic detail. Follow your storyboard closely and keep trying each shot until you get it absolutely perfect!

• Alter the styling as the shoot is in motion. Perfect the look by experimenting with different combinations of accessories and props, but make sure the styling is always obsessively neat.

• Play around with how the models are positioned and try to evoke the same ideas of symmetry, mirroring and reflection in your composition that there is in your styling.

ART vs JEWELLERY

Make priceless jewellery from paper

Check out the queen of art vs jewellery, the super Fred Butler.

Aztec-inspired geometric necklaces, giant 'diamond' rings and never-ending bracelets that coil along the entire length of your arms. Forget conventional jewellery-making techniques like melting metals and laser-cutting plastics, your cosmic jewellery will be sculpted out of the most basic of materials: card. Fill pages of a notebook with the most outlandish and flamboyant jewellery designs. Construct striking statement pieces that belong in the future.

Helpful items

- Felt tips/coloured pencils and paper
- Coloured card – thin enough to fold, thick enough to stand up • Glue/ double-sided sellotape • Scissors • Craft knife • Ruler • Stapler • Elastic • Ribbon • Shoelaces • String

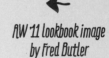

AW '11 lookbook image
by Fred Butler

Step by step

1 Headbands, bracelets, cuffs, tiaras, rings, chokers, necklaces, earrings. Pick a jewellery type and draw out rough designs of what you are going to make. Break down your designs and work out how you will make them. Unless you are prepared for some fiddly work, think big, bold and simple. You may need to make your piece of jewellery in different sections, then stick them together to make the final piece.

2 Choose the colours for your jewellery and start work. Cut out pieces of card to experiment with and try out different approaches to making your jewellery. Don't worry if it takes you a few attempts to work things out. If you are using runny glue, be sparing with it or it can end up all over the place.

3 Once you have made your jewellery, plan your shoot. You could build a small scale set to photograph it in, or you could place it in natural surroundings. Alternatively, ask a friend to model it for you. If you do use a model, be sure to keep the styling simple as the jewellery needs to stand out.

The shoot

- Your jewellery should be the main focus of the shoot! Make sure your model, background or location set a stage for it to shine upon.

- If you are photographing your jewellery on a model, try shooting just the area of the body that the jewellery sits on, e.g. the arm, the neck, or the head.

DAYS GONE BY

Trends don't change every year, every season or every month. What's fashionable and what's not shifts by the second; and only the strongest looks survive. As the years rush by, fashions come and go. Years later when we least expect it, a forgotten look will spring back to steal the stage.

Through the eras we have been hit with some pretty mind-blowing (and a few slightly misguided) trends. To get you in the mood to make a fabulous 'Days Gone By' shoot let's do a quick, retro 'through the years' flashback sequence.

So, there were the...

Rock 'n' roll '50s with poodle skirts, gingham shirts, pastel cardigans, slick quiffs and blood-red lipstick.

Swinging '60s with space-age hot pants, baby doll dresses, geometric shapes, colour clashing, eyeliner flicks and false eyelashes.

Flower power '70s with flowing maxi dresses, wider-than-wide flares, platform shoes, frizzy hair and hand-painted flowers.

Hip hop '80s with over-size sportswear, heavy gold chains, hand-held ghetto blasters, neon baseball caps, braces and big, baggy trousers.

Grungy '90s with ripped drainpipe jeans, oversized woolly jumpers, army jackets, stripey tights, tie-dye and Dr. Martens boots.

*Jordan, c. 1970
by Caroline Greville-Morris*

Step by step

1 Choose a specific era or trend from the past. Which one particularly appeals to you or would be fun to recreate? You may be one of those old souls who has a feeling that you were born in the wrong era. If this is the case, now is your chance to spend a day living the dream.

2 It's time to do some research. What clothing did people wear in your chosen era? How would they have worn their hair and make-up? What accessories would they have had? What was their attitude?

3 Gather together all your inspiration for styling/hair/make-up/photography/art direction by making a moodboard.

*Punk Girls in Hyde Park, 1985
by Gavin Watson*

4 Now it's time to hunt for the perfect clothing for your shoot. Search high and low for the right pieces. Be open to adapting what you find to make it fit the bill.

5 Lastly, scour for locations. Look for public places that have a dated feel e.g. an old laundrette or café. Or keep things simple by using a backdrop.

Helpful items
- Piles of timewarped clothing, accessories and props

The shoot

- To make your model(s) really feel that they belong to the era, get them to become a character from that time. Let's say you have chosen American 1950s housewives. Your 'housewife' will need to pose elegantly and give off a slightly smug 'my life is perfect' vibe. With your models, research how professional models of your chosen time posed in photographs.

- Photographic styles have also changed over time. Early fashion photography from the 1920s is very formal, mostly static and always studio-based. By the time the 1960s arrived, fashion photography had become far more fun and daring, moving out of the studio and onto the street. Try bringing dated photographic styles into your shoot to match your era!

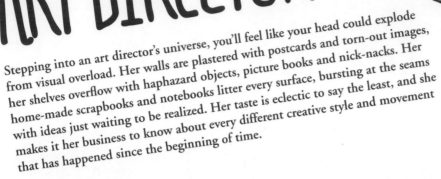

BE AN ART DIRECTOR

Stepping into an art director's universe, you'll feel like your head could explode from visual overload. Her walls are plastered with postcards and torn-out images, her shelves overflow with haphazard objects, picture books and nick-nacks. Her home-made scrapbooks and notebooks litter every surface, bursting at the seams with ideas just waiting to be realized. Her taste is eclectic to say the least, and she makes it her business to know about every different creative style and movement that has happened since the beginning of time.

What do they do?

An art director is responsible for the overall visual theme of the shoot. They work closely with photographers, sharing tasks such as creating storyboards and moodboards, scouting for the right shoot location and working together to cast the models. Then it's up to the art director to source and make props and prepare the set dressing.

On the day of the shoot they work side by side with the photographer, helping direct the shots, suggesting different poses and expressions for the models, changing the location or set and adding or taking away props or objects. They must make decisions to adapt and try out new things, constantly thinking on their feet to keep the shoot on track.

Tips to help you on your way

Build up your own visual reference library. Collect images, make scrapbooks, pick up books and objects that catch your eye. Visit museums and exhibitions and take home postcards of the pieces that excite you.

Start a 'Prop Box'. You never know when you might need a beaten-up old trombone, so grab things when you see them and start your collection now.

Get out and about. Discover interesting and unusual locations for future shoots, recording them all on your camera.

SO HOW DO I DO IT?

Before the shoot

1 Ideas, ideas, ideas! But where do I find them? Work closely with your photographer and start off with some research. Delve into books, magazines and trawl the internet. Make scrapbooks and moodboards to pull together everything you find.

2 Still working with your photographer, translate your research into your own creative ideas for the shoot. Keeping your scrapbooks and moodboards close, move on to making your storyboards.

3 Show the rest of the fashion photography team your moodboards and storyboards. Then let them respond with their own ideas for the styling, make-up and hair.

4 Depending on what your ideas are for the shoot, you may then need to go and scout for locations and make or source props and set dressing.

On the shoot

- Your main job on the shoot day is to set up every scene that is going to be photographed.

- If you are working on a shoot that requires a lot of set dressing, make sure you give yourself bundles of time to set up.

- On the shoot be very, very watchful. Stand next to the photographer, look back at their shots and discuss. What is working or what needs changing?

- As the shoot progresses, try out different set ups. Swap props in and out and if you are shooting on location try out different parts of it.

- Make your models comfortable. Help the photographer direct the models and make them feel relaxed and supported. Suggest different poses and facial expressions, and don't be afraid to jump into the set and show them what you mean.

An art director's toolkit

Props
Set dressing, e.g. various fabrics
Moodboards and storyboards
Notebook and pencil
Point-and-shoot camera
Tape measure
Gaffa tape

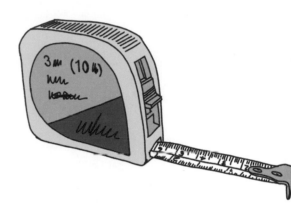

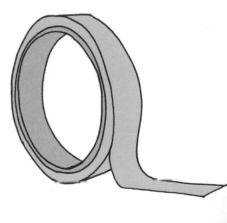

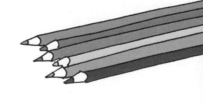

Building Castles in the Sky

Bringing mystery to a shoot is every art director's dream, and with fishing wire this can be achieved in an instant. Fishing wire is an 'invisible string' that is so durable you can hang surprisingly heavy objects from it, it is also very cheap to buy and very easy to use. You will fall in love with it because it gives an illusion that whatever you hang from it is magically floating in mid air. Because you can suspend all kinds of objects with fishing wire it is the ideal material for being inventive. You can make endless sets and backdrops with it, so get hanging, the world is your oyster!

Step by step

1 Firstly, think ideas. What would you like to see suspended in mid air? Or maybe a better question is, what would you *never* see suspended in mid air? Hundreds of pink hearts, old rollerskates, coloured pencils… the options are endless.

2 You can choose to make your hanging objects from scratch or you could use found objects. If you are making your objects, try using card rather than paper as it is far sturdier.

3 Colours. Will you stick to one colour, a range of tones or go all-out with multiple colours? There's no right or wrong when it comes to the colour scheme of your objects, you just need to make a decision and stick to it.

4 Once you have gathered or made your objects, simply cut your fishing wire to the length you want. One by one, tape the fishing wire to the back of each object or tie it around the object.

5 Play around with different ways of hanging your objects. Try suspending them at different heights and depths, as well as experimenting with how you are going to cluster your objects together. Will you hang them in a shape, a line or a group?

6 When you have decided how you want them to hang, just tape the end of the fishing wire to a ceiling in your house, and if you can't reach the ceilings you can always hang your wire in a doorframe.

P.S To avoid peeling the paint off the walls, use drawing pins instead!

- **Fishing wire** (of course) -
N.B. Most hardware shops sell it, or if you know someone
who goes fishing, they will have some you can borrow!
- **Scissors** - **Sellotape/masking tape** -
Electrical tape - **Drawing pins**

← *Inside The Cloud*
by Zim&Zou

Inside The Cloud

The shoot

- Photograph your hanging wonderland from all different angles. Shoot it front-on, lie down underneath it and shoot upwards or stand in the middle of it and shoot all around you! Each position you try will give you a very different result.

- Experiment with your lighting sources and where they are coming from. This will have very different effects on how visible, or invisible, the fishing wire will be in your photographs.

INDOORS OUTDOORS

Indoors outdoors in an invitation to enter into a topsy-turvy world, where nothing is what it should be. Expect to start seeing belongings in the weirdest of places… lampshades hanging from the branches of a tree, an empty baby's cot gently rocking in a field or a carefully laid dining table placed in the middle of a busy street market. Take the indoors outdoors. Move the most everyday objects into the most unlikely locations. Follow in Alice's footsteps and create a wonderland where all is not what it seems…

Step by step

Helpful items
- Furniture of any shape or size
- Little ornaments
- Strong friends

1 Walk around your house and look at everything in it anew. Look for the potential in furniture – there will be items in your house that are just begging to go outside. As well as larger items, look for smaller ornaments. Group these together to make an interesting set of their own, or use them to add detail alongside larger pieces.

2 Once you have identified possible items to use in your shoot, it's time to consider location. Firstly, rack your brains and make a list of all the locations near your house. If you have a garden, don't forget to add it to your list.

3 What kind of setting would really complement or contrast your chosen items? A wildflower meadow or an urban street are both brilliant locations, but they will create very different atmospheres.

4 Now sketch out your storyboards. Plan ideas for how you might go about setting everything up in your location. Be inventive with your set-ups, trying out unusual positions for your pieces – hang things, float things and stand things on end.

The shoot

- This is the hard part: you have to transport everything to your location. Ask friends to join in and help you carry the heavy pieces.

- Try out your different set-ups. Look through your lens to see what really has an impact.

- Once you have set up a shot, shoot it wide to capture the whole scene. After this, zoom in to capture small details.

- It's crucial that you pay attention to everything in your background. Make sure that there is nothing in your frame that shouldn't be there!

Construct
by Agnes Lloyd-Platt

ART DIRECTION

Helpful items
- Fabric – old or new • Sharp scissors • Sewing pins • Needle and thread • Chalk

We've all read enough cheesy slogans to last a lifetime, so it's time to turn things around and make a statement with power and beauty. Your statement doesn't necessarily have to be a full-blown phrase, a single word can carry a punch too. Your words could come from song lyrics, a slogan or you could write your own, but whatever you do, say **SOMETHING**. Now turn your words into a 3D installation. You can make your letters come to life any way you see fit, but to help you on your way, here's how to make some fabric ones…

1 Choose the phrase or word that you want to make. Think of poems, stories, headlines or write some wise words of your own.

2 Grab felt tips and paper and dress your words in the perfect wardrobe. Make your own alphabet any way you want. Mix and match sizes, shapes and styles. Be sure to reflect the sentiment of your words in the colours and fonts you choose. Brave words would suit bright neons and angular shapes while wistful words that would suit pastel shades and swirly shapes.

3 Count your letters and decide how big you want them to be. With this in mind, gather enough fabric to make them. Hunt through drawers at home or hit the shops to source something specific.

4 Make your letters. Lay your fabric out on a table or on the floor. Cut as many equal-sized rectangles as you have letters. Next, pick up a rectangle and fold it in half. This will make the front and the back of the letter. Pin the edges roughly together to keep the letter in place.

5 Use some chalk to lightly sketch out your first letter onto the square.

6 Cut out the letter shape, making sure you are cutting through both layers of the folded fabric. Now you have two of the same letter.

7 Lay one letter shape on top of the other and pin around them. Hand-sew them together or use a sewing machine. Don't sew them up completely! Remember to leave a hand-sized gap so that you can stuff the letter.

8 Turn your letter inside out to get clean edges and to hide where you have sewn the pieces together.

9 Grab some old fabric or scrunched-up newspaper and stuff it through the gap to make your letter 3D. Push your stuffing in firmly, packing it in tightly to make it solid and sturdy.

10 Once you have stuffed your letter, sew up the gap. Repeat these steps for each letter until your statement is made.

The shoot

- Think of different settings and locations for your word(s) to be photographed in. Try shooting them indoors, outdoors, on the bus, viewed through a window, floating off into the sky tied to balloons…

- You need to be able to fit the whole phrase in your frame, which can be tricky if the phrase is long. If it is, find a location that has enough room for you to stand far back so that you can squeeze it all in.

↓

Jump For My Love
by Ichbinkong

THE POLKA DOT ROOM

Japanese artist Yayoi Kusama's wonderful polka dot room is creativity at its finest. Brightly coloured polka dots casually lie on every surface of this white room. Look closely and you'll see that these colourful polka dots aren't a trick of the eye or computer-generated; they are just cut-out shapes that have been stuck on to everything. Just a genius idea and one simple cut-out shape is all it takes to give a location an unbelievable transformation.

Step by step

1 Firstly, choose a room. Grab your camera, tour your house, and pick somewhere that has lots of natural light. If you can't find a room that does, bring in lots of lamps or use your camera's flash.

2 Move furniture and objects around in the room until you have the perfect setting.

3 Next, think about the shapes and colours that will transform your room. Stars, circles, hearts, question marks, squares… or a repeat pattern of a couple together. One colour or multi-colour? The choice is yours.

4 Create a template of your shape(s). Make it out of card, then you can draw around it to keep all your shapes uniform. Draw around it to make as many shapes as possible. Grab your scissors and cut them out.

5 Play around with where you place the shapes in the room. Jump in and get started, dotting your shapes around. Lay them on surfaces as well as using blu-tack to attach them to objects and the walls.

6 Once you are satisfied with the amount of shapes scattered around, set up your camera and look at the scene you have created. You'll see gaps that need filling and places where there are too many clustered together. Re-arrange the scene until you are 100 per cent happy, then you can begin shooting.

The Obliteration Room
by Yayoi Kusama, installation at the
Gallery of Modern Art, Brisbane

Helpful items
- Coloured paper or card
- Scissors • Blu-tack

The shoot

- You may need to stand right back against the wall to fit everything into your frame. Try standing in a doorway if you're tight on space or alternatively focus on only one area of your room.

- Once you have captured the whole set-up, play around with your zoom and photograph smaller areas within your scene.

BE A
PHOTOGRAPHER

A fashion photographer spends their time shooting from dusk 'til dawn, stopping only when they are satisfied that they have created the most beautiful images imaginable. After any shoot you'll find them huddled over a computer, excitedly editing their photographs. In their spare time, they're either on the look-out for super-cool shoot locations, geeking-out over camera equipment or trawling through blogs, magazines and books hunting for inspiration for their next shoot…

What do they do?

Some people think that all a fashion photographer does is click their camera at a pouting model dressed head-to-toe in designer clothing. However, *extra*-ordinary fashion photography is made by true artists with vision. For them fashion photography is a place where they can create playful and magical worlds in which anything can happen. Often fashion photographers work closely with the art director.

Fashion photographers must obviously perfect their photography skills, but just as importantly, they need to develop their own photographic style. A great fashion photographer's work needs its own voice. Finding that voice is the hard part. Trying out different ideas and playing with photographic styles is the way to discover it. Then it's time to practise it.

Tips to help you on your way

Research fashion photographers through the ages, up to the present day. Collect images of their work.

Think about creating your own distinctive style so that your work stands out from the crowd.

Learning how to control exposure, shutter speeds and aperture will give you control over how your photographs come out. Look up video tutorials online for these technicalities.

SO HOW DO I DO IT?

1 Get your hands on a camera. It doesn't have to be expensive. Use an SLR, digital compact, disposable camera or even a camera phone.

2 Whether you are working with an art director or going solo, decide upon a theme, location and atmosphere for your fashion shoot. Create moodboards to lock down your ideas.

3 Location. Work out where you want to shoot your fashion story – outside or inside? Are you setting up a backdrop, a room inside your home or using a public location outside, like a street market?

4 Storyboard your ideas for each shot you want to capture in your fashion shoot. Ask yourself the following questions:

How will you compose and frame each shot?
What will your models be doing?
What will their facial expressions be?
What angles will you will be shooting from?

5 Whatever your camera, make sure to charge it the night before the shoot. Clean your lens/es! Always pack your charger and spare memory cards/film just in case you need them.

A fashion photographer's toolkit

- A camera. This can be a phone camera, disposable camera, a high-tech SLR camera or an old film camera. All will give you different looking photographs, but the main thing is that you just need a camera of some kind to shoot on. You can always start on an inexpensive camera and move up-market when the time comes.

- A lens cloth, or just a piece of clean fabric to clean off any smears on your lens.

- A reflector. This is a reflective surface that is used to redirect light towards your model. Use a big white piece of card or buy a specially made one from a photographic shop.

- Investing in a separate flash or photographic lights is a great idea farther down the road. They are expensive but they will give you more control over lighting your shoots and give dramatic results too.

On the shoot

- While the models are getting ready, go through your storyboards with the art director to set up your first shot.

- Before you start shooting your way through your storyboards, take a test shot of the model in the first position. Show it to the rest of the team to check that you are all happy with the lighting, styling, make-up and set dressing. When everyone is happy, then you can begin.

- Always try different compositions – shoot from below, above and to the side of your model and give them clear direction at all times.

- Work on each shot until you think you have the perfect photograph. Take your time rather than rushing through your shots. It's better to have a few exceptional photographs from a shoot than hundreds that aren't quite right.

HIT THE ROAD JACK

'Hit the Road Jack' indulges the explorer in us all, whispering words of encouragement to our inner free spirit. Pack a bag, grab your camera and hit that road. Seek out and discover forgotten atmospheric places that are overlooked by everyone else: a derelict lighthouse, an abandoned petrol station, an overgrown tennis court, an old-fashioned lido. Explore, discover and go where no one else has gone before. The location you choose will dictate the entire idea, theme, look and feel of your fashion shoot, so pick wisely…

Helpful items

- You already know… an incredible location

Hotel by Cari Ann Wayman

Two Guns by Cari Ann Wayman

1 This shoot is about being brave and getting out there. Explore places that you already know of, as well as letting yourself dream of locations that you have never been to yet. Make a list of all the different types of location that might inspire you: old caravan parks, shopping centres, botanical gardens… Review your list and divide the locations into two groups: An 'EASY' list for locations that you already know, and that would be easy to shoot at. e.g. a local games arcade. A 'HARD' list for locations that are pie-in-the-sky dreams e.g. a castle.

2 Now, decide what level of challenge you are up for! Either choose a location that's on the 'easy' list, or pick one from the 'hard' list.

3 When you settle upon somewhere, you may need to ask permission to photograph there. Get in touch and explain that you would love to do a shoot there. Offer them a few photographs from the shoot as this may help to get a yes!

4 Once you have your location, brainstorm ideas around it. Let the location filter into every detail of the shoot – from what the models will be doing, to the make-up design to the styling theme.

5 Visit your location (known in the trade as, 'doing a recce'). Check out every part of it, leave no door unopened or corner undiscovered. With an art director's eye, scout out the most interesting parts of the location to shoot in. Checking it out will give you an idea of how your shoot could work. Then storyboard out your shots.

6 Preparation is key for a location shoot, because if you forget anything on the day, you're scuppered. Pack absolutely EVERYTHING – and make sure your camera is FULLY charged.

7 Grab your storyboards and your bursting bags and head out!

The shoot

- You might not be the only people at your location, there may well be other members of the public around. Keep an eye on the background when you are shooting to ensure you don't get a stray person in the shot that you don't want! Be inventive with how you capture the location. Take wide shots to capture your whole location as well as close-ups that give just a hint of it.

- Be adaptable! Shooting on location always brings up a whole lot of unknowns that you can't prepare for. Roll with the punches, think on your feet and use your creativity to rethink your shoot if need be!

FOLLOW IN THEIR FOOTSTEPS

Iconic fashion photographers tend to have an individual style so distinct that we can recognize their work as soon as we stumble across it. Now it's your chance to mix your fresh talent with an iconic image and see what you get.

Find a photographer whose work you adore, select your all-time favourite image and re-create it adding your very own personal twist. There are hoards of mind-blowing fashion photographers to choose from, from Louise Dahl Wolfe's elegant, art-inspired shoots to Sarah Moon's dreamworld fantasies.

Another example is Elaine Constantine, whose 'Girls on Bikes' image can be seen opposite. Her photograph bursts with movement, fun, energy and youthfulness – and the models wear fantastic facial expressions. If you were to choose to mimic Elaine's photograph, you could keep a similar location by finding a hill, but change the action and the styling. So your shot could involve a group of 'mod-styled' boys sprinting down the hill screaming into the lens. You've captured Elaine's youthful energy but definitely added your own signature to the shoot.

Step by step

1 Scour the internet or a big bookshop looking for your perfect photographer.

2 Make sure that you choose a photographer whose work isn't too complicated to replicate. For example, if a photographer's work relies on high-tech computer manipulation or they always shoot in far-away locations, you may have to reconsider your choice!

3 Once you have chosen a photographer look really closely through their work and choose one photograph that really grabs you. What makes it stand out? Is it the subject matter, the lighting, the styling or the composition? These are the key things that you need to bring into your own shoot

4 Start storyboarding your ideas. It's up to you whether you would like to recreate the image, or go for an 'inspired by' shoot. Be playful with what you choose to swap or switch. Even the slightest change to the raw ingredients of a photograph can have a massive impact on the outcome!

The shoot

- As you are shooting, check that your photographs are capturing the desired effect that you have planned. If not, stop, reconsider and begin again until the photographs are working to your satisfaction!

- Keep the image you are recreating on you so that you can refer to it throughout the shoot. Glance at it and then at your images to keep you on track.

Girls On Bikes
by Elaine Constantine

Say Cheese!

Getting the best out of your models on a fashion shoot takes a little more directing than just mouthing 'say cheese!' at them across the set. Learning how to direct a model into the most striking and evocative poses takes skill and imagination. Grab a model and click your way through these sequences. By the time you reach the end, you will be a master at directing.

Helpful items
- A camera • A model

Kodak Girl, 1896

Pearls of wisdom

While you are concentrating on directing your model you also need to think about the angles you are shooting from. Shoot from all different positions; from below, up high, to the left of your model and to the right. Go wide and shoot full-body, crop half body and zoom in and take close-ups too.

When you are shooting your sequences, don't expect to get the perfect shot first time, keep directing the model as you go along until you get shots you are happy with.

When you have finished shooting, go through all of your shots carefully. Think about which ones work best and why.

The sequences

With the sequences below by your side, ask your model to really…

Get emotional

Smiling – giggling – laughing out loud – hysterically laughing
Sad – tearful – totally heartbroken

Get moving

Walking – skipping – running – jumping – spinning

Give you a perfect profile

Front-on – turn to the right – turn to the left – look over your shoulder

Show you their soul

Look right into the camera – look up – look off-camera – look down at the floor

Get comfortable

Standing – kneeling – sitting – lying – sleeping

Step by step

1 Grab a model. Forget about the styling, hair and make-up. Keep your model neutral. We're talking jeans and a white T-shirt. A bit boring we know, but for this to work their appearance needs to blend in rather than dominate the photographs.

2 The best location for this shoot is a simple brick wall or anywhere there isn't a lot going on in the background. Again, this will keep the focus on the actions, rather than what's going on in the background.

3 Right, you've got your model and the location sorted. With the sequences above by your side ask your model to really, really go for it as you direct them into each position. Remember to make your model feel comfortable and relaxed while you are photographing them. You will only get the best out of them if they trust you and feel you are being supportive. Getting frustrated with your model if you are having trouble getting the shots won't help!

365
DAYS OF
FASHION

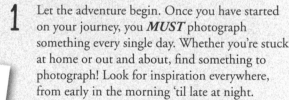

THURSDAY 30TH MARCH

FRIDAY 31ST MARCH

'Fashion is not something that exists in dresses only. Fashion is in the sky, in the street. Fashion has to do with ideas, the way we live, what is happening.'
Coco Chanel

There are 365 days in a year. Starting from today, every single day for the next year photograph something that could inspire a fashion shoot. As Coco wisely reminds us, fashion is all around us; where you choose to see it is up to you. An electric blue plastic bag blowing in the wind, fresh white blossom on the branches of an apple tree, reflections in a Christmas tree bauble, a tiny chihuahua in his spring raincoat or a beautiful, effervescent rainbow.

Come rain or come shine keep snapping every day and by the end of the year you will have an incredible archive of 365 days of fashion.

→

Images by Lisa Comeford,
Elle Benton at Yellow Bird
Photography, and
Tita Beaufrand

SATURDAY 1ST

SUNDAY 2ND APRIL

Step by step

1 Let the adventure begin. Once you have started on your journey, you **MUST** photograph something every single day. Whether you're stuck at home or out and about, find something to photograph! Look for inspiration everywhere, from early in the morning 'til late at night.

2 To do this you need some kind of camera on you AT ALL TIMES. If it's not practical to keep your camera with you, shoot on a camera phone.

3 Start an online diary for your shots, e.g. an Instagram, Flickr, blog or Pinterest account. This way you can upload your 365 Days of Fashion and see how your archive is developing. You can also invite others to follow your progress.

4 Don't give up! This isn't always going to be an easy diary to keep but it is the best way to keep your inspiration flowing, ideas bubbling and photography skills developing, so stay on it.

MONDAY 3RD APRIL

TUESDAY 4TH APRIL

WEDNESDAY 5TH APRIL

FRIDAY 7TH APRIL

THURSDAY 6TH APRIL

SATURDAY 8TH APRIL

SUNDAY 9TH APRIL

MONDAY 10TH APRIL

Teenagers Dancing and
Listening to Rock 'n' Roll On
the Beach by Lynn Pelham

Perfect Props

Big, Beautiful Bows

Say no to shop-bought accessories and let big, hand-made bows work their simple magic. The perfect adornment for any hairstyle, big, beautiful bows love to be made in any design, in any colour and adore being the centre of attention.

You will need

- A sheet of coloured foam (Any size will do. The bigger, the better) • Coloured electrical tape • Kirby grips • Stickers of any kind (optional)

Step by step

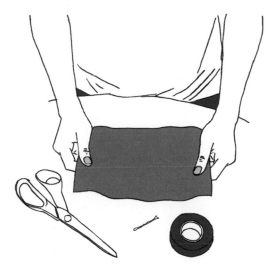

1 Take a sheet of foam and grab your scissors and tape.

2 Concertina the foam.

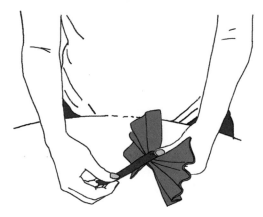

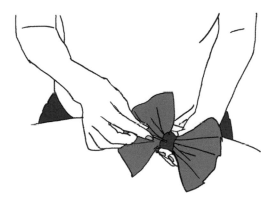

3 Take a piece of electrical tape and neatly tape around the middle

4 Slip one side of the kirby grip behind the tape, so that it can be worn in the hair

Don't stop at one bow, create a collection. Mix and match the colours of your foam and decorate with different kinds of stickers.

My Bunny Rabbit Glasses
Inspired by Peter Jensen

Hopping off the catwalk and into your hands, here's how to make your own bunny rabbit glasses inspired by brilliant fashion designer Peter Jensen! They couldn't be easier to make or more fun to wear.

Step by step

1 Cut out the template.

2 Lay the template on top of the card from which you are going to make your bunny rabbit glasses.

3 Draw around the template.

4 Cut carefully around your pencil outline.

5 Cut out the windows in the glasses where the lenses go.

6 That's it… your bunny rabbit glasses are ready to go.

You will need
- Coloured card - Scissors
- A pencil - A pair of sunglasses - Blu-tack

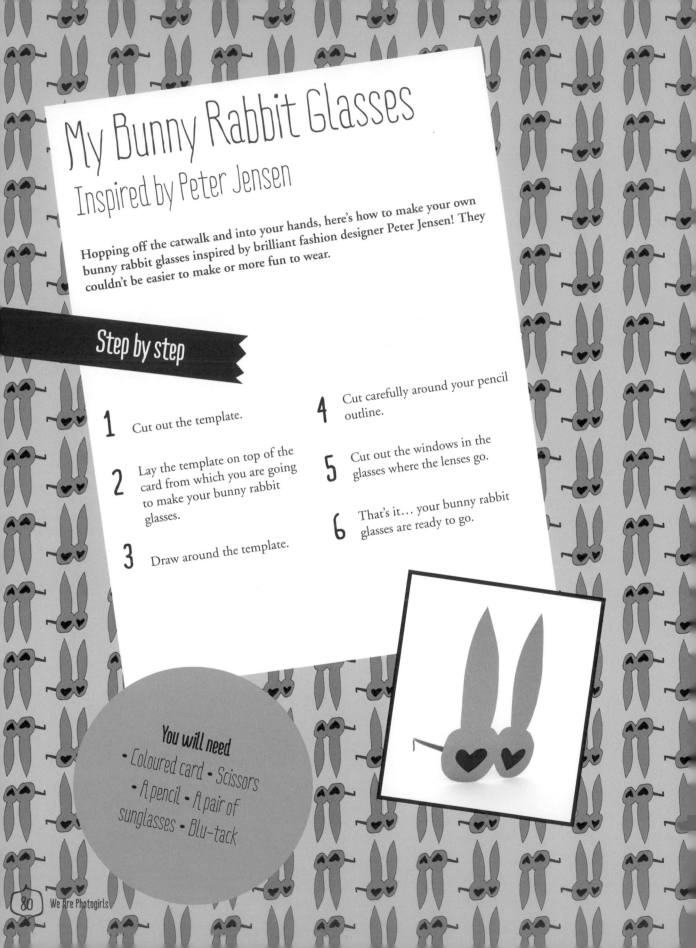

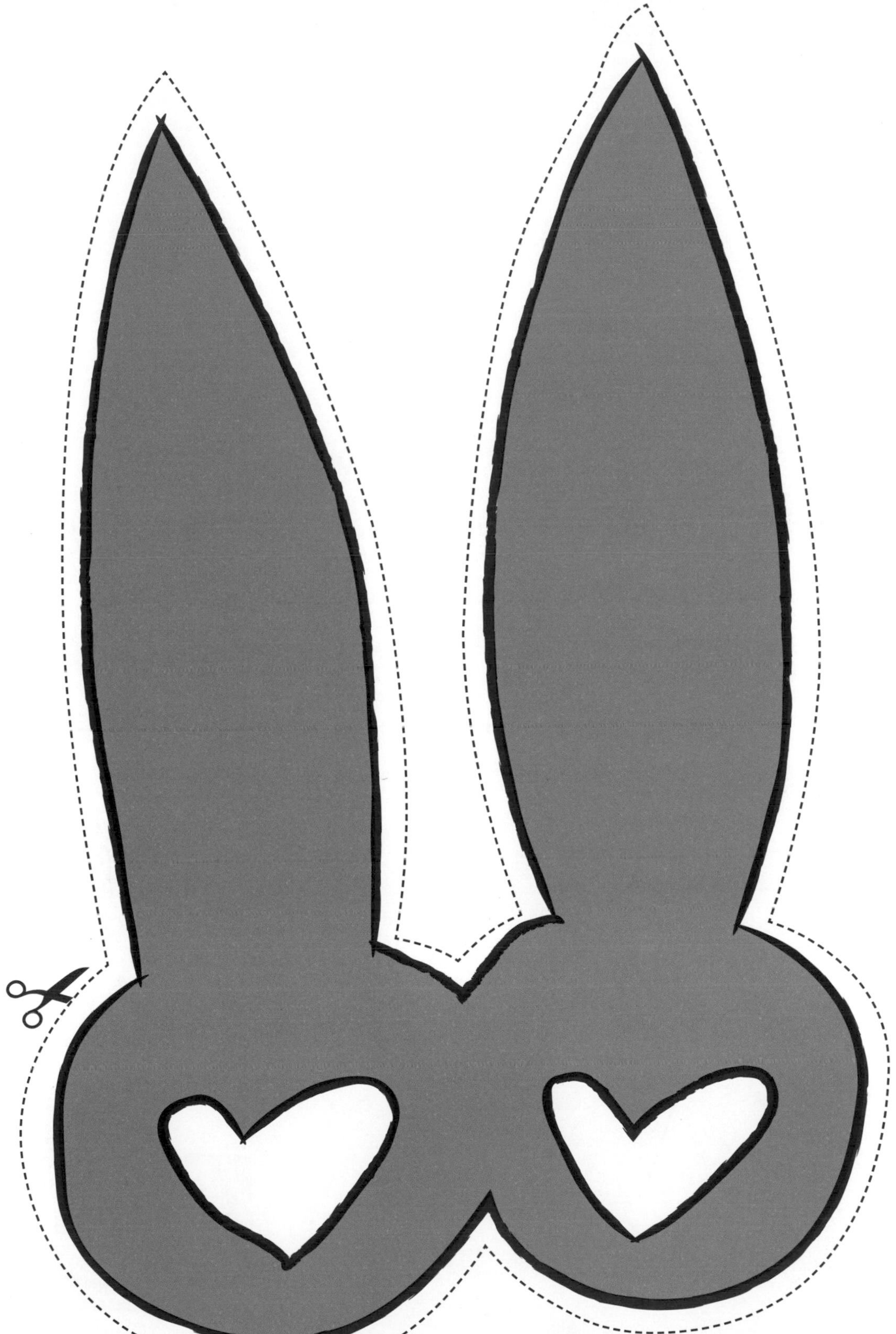

Neon Ghetto-blaster

This is a ghetto-blaster like no other that will steal the limelight of any shoot with its loud 1980s looks. Rest it on your shoulder and let it speak for itself.

Step by step

1 Take a big sheet of card. Draw and cut out your basic ghetto-blaster shape.

2 Add speakers! Cut out startburst shapes and stick to either side of the tape deck.

3 Make your tape deck. Cut out two rectangles, one bigger than the other out of different colours. See the drawing below for a scale guide. Glue on your tape deck.

4 Customize your ghetto-blaster if you so desire, adding designs and function buttons.

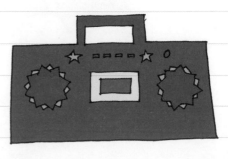

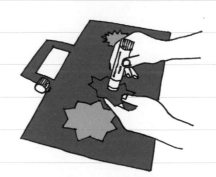

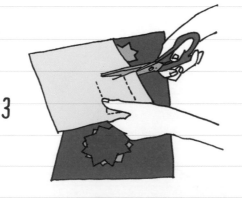

You will need
- 2–3 sheets of neon card in different colours (any size between A4–A1)
- Pritt stick
- Scissors • Ruler

Giant Pom-poms

Brighten the universe and fill every inch of it with giant, colourful pom-poms. Cut, concertina and fan your way through sheets and sheets of tissue paper and never be stuck for a set or a prop again…

You will need

• At least 10 sheets of tissue paper (the more sheets, the bigger the pom-pom.) • Scissors • A rubber band • Fishing wire

Step by step

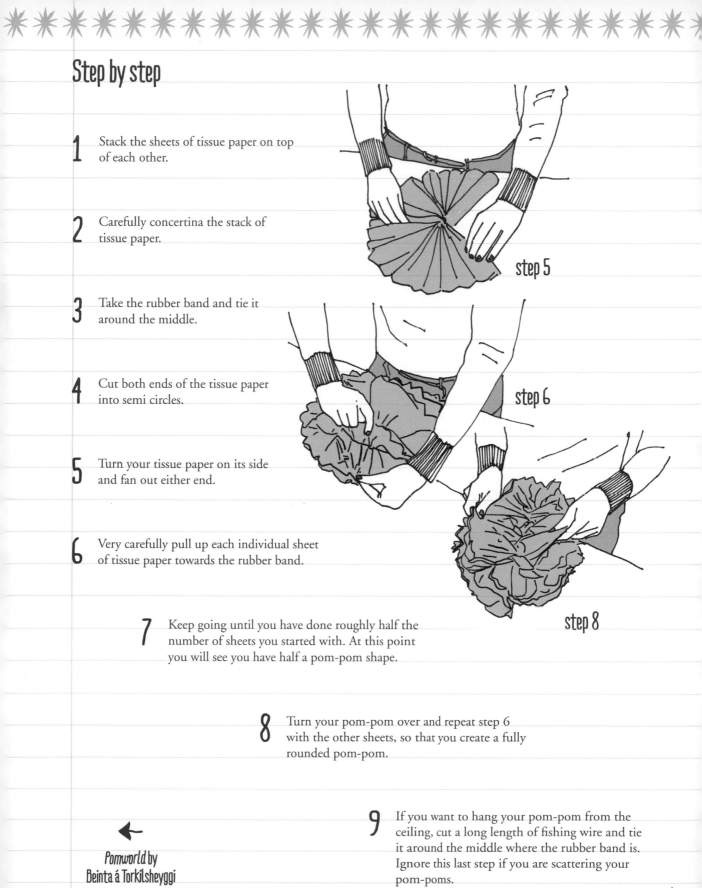

1   Stack the sheets of tissue paper on top of each other.

2   Carefully concertina the stack of tissue paper.

3   Take the rubber band and tie it around the middle.

4   Cut both ends of the tissue paper into semi circles.

5   Turn your tissue paper on its side and fan out either end.

6   Very carefully pull up each individual sheet of tissue paper towards the rubber band.

7   Keep going until you have done roughly half the number of sheets you started with. At this point you will see you have half a pom-pom shape.

8   Turn your pom-pom over and repeat step 6 with the other sheets, so that you create a fully rounded pom-pom.

9   If you want to hang your pom-pom from the ceiling, cut a long length of fishing wire and tie it around the middle where the rubber band is. Ignore this last step if you are scattering your pom-poms.

step 5

step 6

step 8

←
Pomworld by
Beinta á Torkilsheyggi

Post Up a Post-it

It's so simple, the Post-it backdrop doesn't actually need any introduction; but how spectacular does it look? Cover the entire wall or plaster smaller areas to create patterns. It's a perfect backdrop for an unusual fashion shoot; go Post-it crazy.

Step by step

1 Choose an area of wall to make your backdrop on. Make sure the area is wide enough to fit a person in front.

2 Open your Post-it notes. Before you begin sticking them up, decide upon your design or colour scheme. You could keep it simple by sticking different colours next to each other to make checks or stripes, or get more complicated and make letters or shapes.

3 Make sure that your Post-it notes are right next to each other so there are no gaps in between them.

4 Start sticking at the centre of the wall and work outwards.

5 You're done! If you make any mistakes, just take up the Post-it notes and re-stick.

You will need
- A few packs of multi-coloured Post-it notes • A plain wall

Mixte editorial 2 image/stage
by Sandra Freij

A Whole Day To Fill

THE NEW DESIGNERS ARE HERE

Make something that has never been seen before! Create an outfit. Not just any outfit. An outfit that is totally and utterly unique. Either design completely from scratch or find a piece of old clothing and transform it into something fit for the catwalk. A simple construction can be as striking as a complicated one, so don't panic if you can't even thread a needle. Look at the incredible designers featured: Robin Lasser's fantastic tent dress and Madame Peripetie's wonderful blue creature show us how to think outside the box. Remember, you are designing a piece of art: indulging your imagination is the key to success.

Steps for making from scratch

1 Think materials and objects. Look around your home for unusual possibilities. You don't have to stick to traditional fabrics, you can make something out of anything. You could use tennis balls, paper plates or even an old tent... so get hunting!

2 If you are feeling stuck for ideas, look at your fabric or materials. Let them be your guiding inspiration. Pick them up and play around with them. Don't get too analytical, just experiment. Trying out different things will help you to find out what really works.

3 Sketch out your design. Once you have the general feel, think about little details that could make your outfit truly distinctive.

4 Now it's time to take the plunge and start cutting up your materials. If you are using fabric, allow more material than you think you will need. Make sure you don't get caught out with too little!

5 If you need to attach materials together, look at their textures. Can you sew through them with a big needle and strong thread? Can you staple into them or will glue or sticky tabs stick them together?

Steps for customizing

1 Have a good rummage through your wardrobe for an old item of clothing to customize. Go for something with a fabric you like as you can change the shape or cut.

2 Look at your chosen item. How can you reinvent it? Remember, your item doesn't even need to be worn in the way it was originally designed. You could turn that ill-fitting ski suit into a geometric, tailored evening jacket with matching clutch bag.

Picnic Dress Tent by Robin Lasser and Adrienne Pao

Final steps for both

- If you are planning to photograph your outfit on a model you need to guarantee that it will fit, so get them to try it on while you make it.

- Last but not least, make accessories to match your outfit. These will give your design a unity and could be as simple as tying leftover material into a makeshift headband or cuff.

DIY research

Be inspired by designers Maison Martin Margiela, Maria Blaisse and Hussein Chalayan.

Here are a few tricks that can rapidly transform an old item:

- Drastically change the neckline
- Add billowing sleeves or rip off the existing ones
- Add over-the-top length that trails across the floor
- Go 'giant puffball' by adding layer upon layer of fabric
- Add details such as lace, buttons or embroidery
- P.S. Don't throw away any leftover fabric. This can be used to make a belt, bow or a rosette.

Cleaner | pugh-atory | 2010
by Madame Peripetie

Helpful items

- Safety pins/normal pins • Sewing needles & thread • PVA glue or a glue gun • A stapler and lots of staples • Double-sided sticky tabs • A pair of sharp scissors • A sewing machine

The shoot

Now you have completed your outfit it's time to shoot it.

- Either ask a friend to model it for you or find an atmospheric setting for your creation to live in. You could try hanging it up high, draping it over a gorgeously painted cupboard or letting it float in a bath.

- If you are using a model make sure that they are styled from head-to-toe and don't forget to think about their hair and make-up too.

- Make the most of your design. Madame Peripetie's vision has become more than just an outfit in the photograph because the hair, make-up and styling has transformed the model into a character fit for a modern-day fairy tale.

Pearls of wisdom

- Don't fret too much if you can't make a piece that will last forever. It only needs to last long enough to be documented in your shoot.

- If you are using more than one fabric, think about how the colours and patterns look together.

- If you have worked hard on intricate details, or have designed your own accessories, be sure to zoom in and get some close-up shots of them.

- Encourage your model to interact with the outfit. This can create interesting shapes and bring movement into your photographs.

Food Glorious Food

Remember what you did with food when you were a kid? You never just ate it – you had fun with it, drew with it, built with it, even wore it!

Food Glorious Food is an invitation to revive your forgotten playfulness with food. Fish, doughnuts, watermelons, baked beans, bananas, carrots, marshmallows, candy floss… build fantastical sets with it, squash it into accessories, mould it into hats and glasses, cover your body in it and hang it from the ceilings. Unleash food in all its glory.

There are two ways to approach this shoot:

Option one is to investigate your kitchen, see what you've got in your cupboards and let your findings dictate your brainstorming.

Option two is to think the other way round. Start off by brainstorming ideas. Think of foods that might be exciting to work with or that look fantastic then hit the shops with your shopping list!

P.S. Don't forget that food packaging can look great too. Brightly decorated cereal packets, for example, can be just as inspiring as the food inside them.

Step by step

1 Sketch out and moodboard your ideas. Think about the colours, textures and personalities of your chosen foods. How can you wear it, style it, make patterns with it or build with it? Imagine a bow tie sculpted from cabbage leaves or statement jewellery carved from raw vegetables.

2 Storyboard 1-5 scenarios. There is so much you can do with food there is no excuse not to bother with your storyboards. With your model(s), roll in it, throw it, jump on it, eat it or juggle with it.

3 If you are working hands-on with the food, a big clear table or the floor works well. Be sure to spread out some bin bags or old tablecloths to work on.

4 Attaching foods together ain't easy. Use anything you can think of that may work. Soft stuff can be sewed through, whereas hard stuff can be stuck together with sticky tabs or glue.

5 Once you've got to grips with your food creations, make sure your model(s) are styled and made up to match. If you're covering them with food, be sure to get the set ready before you plaster them!

DIY research

Watch the original 1971 *Willy Wonka's Chocolate Factory* for sickly sweet art direction.

Gawp in amazement at the world's biggest food fight. La Tomatina Festival in Spain.

Be inspired by artists Bompas and Parr's wonderful jelly sculptures.

The shoot

- What location will you use to photograph your shoot? If you have built a set, where will you place it? If you are using your food to tell a fashion story, does it need to be told in a specific setting?

- Play around with how the food is positioned within your frame. Don't just stick to one composition, try out all different options. This is the only way to ensure exciting and unexpected results.

- Shoot through the food for unusual compositions!

Fairy Bread
by The Girls

Helpful items
- Food • Bin bags, tablecloths or anything that will protect your surfaces from sticky mess

THE WONDERFUL WORLD OF PINHOLE CAMERAS

Take a photograph with a pinhole camera and it will look nothing like a 'normal' photograph. With a dreamy, haunting quality it's a throwback to the adventurous days of early Victorian photography. The wonderful world of pinhole cameras is daring, unpredictable, thrilling and full of surprises. Who would have thought this was possible from a camera that you can make yourself? You never know how things will turn out with a pinhole – every photograph is an experiment and once you embrace their whimsical nature you'll never look back…

Pinhole cameras are the most basic and simple cameras in existence. Made out of only three things (a **lightproof box**, photo paper and a **pinhole**) the pinhole, as its name suggests, is made with a pin. This hole allows daylight to stream into the box and land on the light-sensitive photo paper. This is how the photograph is made.

Girl at Listening Vessel by
Diana Hooper Bloomfield

Step by step

Making your camera

1 Firstly you need to black out the inside and outside of the box. Either paint it or use black sugar paper or foil to carefully cover every inch of it. Make sure that everything is blacked out once you have finished.

2 Cut a hole in the centre of one of the sides of your box (about the size of a ping-pong ball).

3 Next, cut out a piece of black paper or foil big enough to easily cover the hole you have just made.

4 With your needle or pin slowly push a hole into the centre of the black paper or foil you have just cut out. You need a nice clean hole that will let the light through.

5 Now firmly tape this piece of paper or foil over the hole that you have cut in the box. Make sure the pinhole is in the middle of the hole in the box so the light can get through and into the box.

6 Cut out another small piece of paper or foil the same size as the last one. This will act as a cover for the pinhole. Tape it on top of the pinhole. Don't stick it on too firmly as you will need to untape it to expose your pinhole to the light and then tape it shut again to block it out.

Complete this last step in total darkness!

7 Never take your photo paper out of its packaging unless you are in complete darkness, so shut yourself in a darkened room or wardrobe. Cut out a rectangle of photo paper that will fit the inside wall of your box (this should be the opposite wall to your pinhole.) Blu-tack the paper to the wall. The glossy side of the paper should face outwards.

Now you are ready to shoot!

DIY research

- Be inspired by Worldwide Pinhole Photography Day and send in your entries
- Gawp in amazement at the thousands of pinhole photographs on Flickr's Pinhole Photography group

Helpful items

• A sturdy box with a tight-fitting lid, for example, a shoebox. • Tape • Blu-tack • Either black, non- glossy paint, black sugar paper or aluminium foil • Scissors or a Stanley knife • Sharp pin or needle • Glossy light-sensitive photographic paper (Order online in all different sizes, in colour or black and white. N.B. inkjet photo paper won't work!) • A stopwatch or timer • A sunny day

The shoot

- Your pinhole camera will only work on a sunny day. Check the weather forecast in advance.

- As this process is a new one, test out your pinhole camera before your fashion shoot to make sure you have got the hang of it.

- Do a test shot on something static like a tree or a building. When you are ready to take your photograph, you must only let light through your pinhole for a controlled amount of time. Lift up the cover and expose the pinhole. The right amount of time ranges from between 2-16 seconds. Choose something in between to begin with, say 9 seconds.

- After you have taken your photograph you need to take your paper out in TOTAL darkness again! When you take it out, store it carefully in a lightproof bag, e.g. a black bin bag tied tightly. Then reload for your next shot.

- Repeat this process trying out a few test shots with different times to see what works best.

- Photographing a fashion shoot on a pinhole camera can create wonderful results but you have to be particularly patient. When you are ready to photograph a fashion shoot on one, make sure your model is in a comfortable position because it is going to take time to get the shots right.

- When your shoot is over, hurry down to your nearest photographic shop and drop of your lightproof bag to be developed. It's exciting counting down the seconds 'til pick-up time!

Pearls of wisdom

Unlike a digital camera, with a pinhole camera you have absolutely no idea how your photographs are going to turn out. Take a few more shots than you think you need, to make sure you get the photographs you want.

The bigger the pinhole camera, the bigger the photo you can take. With Xtra large photo paper go huge by making a giant pinhole out of an enormous cardboard box!

CINEMATIK

Get cosy on the sofa, tuck into some fresh popcorn and indulge in back-to-back films. Tune into old black and white love stories, sing-a-long musicals, the latest Hollywood blockbusters and rare art-house movies.

Immerse yourself in all things cinematic, sifting through the never-ending inspiration found beyond the silver screen. A film has so many places for you to search for ideas. The plot, the title, the characters or a film's visual style can all fill you with ideas for an Oscar-worthy fashion shoot.

Pearls of wisdom

As there are literally thousands and thousands of films to choose from, you may feel a little overwhelmed on where to start looking. A good way to break films down is by choosing from a genre. e.g. Spaghetti Western, Disney cartoons or Hammer Horror.

To get a quick feel for a film, watch the trailer on the internet.

Don't just copy the film's wardrobe, add your own personal touches.

Helpful items
- DVDs - A comfy sofa
- Some tasty snacks
- A notebook and pen

'War' by Tejal Patni

Step by step

Pick your inspiration film. You could choose a firm favourite that you have watched a million times or borrow some DVDs and discover something new. Settle down with a notebook to watch them, hitting pause and jotting down anything that grabs your attention. It could be a scene that is a visual masterpiece, characters that are beautifully styled, or a thrilling story line.

1 Now brainstorm your ideas into a full-blown shoot. Your shoot doesn't have to be a carbon copy of the film you choose, it just needs to be *inspired* by it. Make a moodboard to help you work out how you would like the shoot to look and feel.

2 Move on to storyboarding your ideas, drawing out 1– 4 shots. As well as thinking about the styling, art direction, make-up and hair design you will also need to think about your location. Make a set or hunt for a location inspired by those in the film.

3 Make a list of all the items you need for the shoot – from specific lipstick shades to accessories that need to be made. Make sure you gather together and make all your items before your shoot.

4 Style and make-up your model(s) and you're ready to go.

The shoot

- As your shoot is inspired by the cinema, think like a filmmaker. You want your shots to be as slick and well-crafted as a cinematic masterpiece so follow your story-boards to the tiniest detail.

- Atmospheric lighting is crucial in the cinema, so experiment with different lighting yourself. Try turning out all the lights and using torches or bringing lots of lamps in to light your scene. Coloured lightbulbs can add an interesting effect too, so have a go with these.

- Get your models thinking like actors, asking them to play a character or a role. The best way to capture drama is to have the model(s) play out a scene, and then shout 'freeze' when you want to shoot.

DIY research

- Fall in love with super-kitch '60s styling in Bollywood blockbuster *Mughal-E-Azam*.
- Gawp in amazement at the pop cinematography in Baz Luhrmann's *Romeo + Juliet*.
- Listen to the cheesy soundtrack from the 1978 high-school movie *Grease*.

➤

Still from Robert Siodmak's film *The Spiral Staircase* starring Dorothy McGuire

Off the Top of Your Head

This shoot is your chance to turn traditional millinery* on its head. You are going to make a piece of headwear like no other. To make this show-stopping piece you are going to have to start thinking outside the box.

Take a look at the toy jungle in Piers Atkinson's 'Fauna'. We love it. It is playful and inventive and very simple. Throw yourself head first into the art of millinery and you'll never look back…

Millinery is the art of designing and making women's hats.

Step by step

1 Let your imagination run free and get drawing. Sketch, design and brainstorm as this will really help you to figure out how your creation will look, and how you will practically make it. The essential design problem you will have to solve is how you will make your headpiece wearable. Think about what you might be able to use as a base for it; hats, visors, Alice bands and headbands could all be adapted to help you get started.

2 Think about what kinds of materials you will use. For example, let's say that you wanted to make a headdress out of playing cards. Would you use real playing cards, or would you hand-make them because you want them to be abnormally huge and have a home-made look?

3 Gather together all the materials you are going to need so they are ready for the making!

4 Play around with your materials and test out different ways of joining them together – try glue, sticky tape, staples, etc. This will help you to find the most efficient way of making your piece secure.

5 If you are using heavy objects in your design, weight will be your biggest enemy. What if you have decided to build a piece of headwear out of china cups? The base needs to be really sturdy to handle this weight! A flimsy sun hat won't do, you will need a stronger hat. When an architect designs a building, they build solid foundations to guarantee that it won't topple over. Your situation is exactly the same!

Unititled by William Selden

Helpful items

- PVA glue • Blu-Tack • Needle and thread • Sticky fasteners • Velcro • A stapler • Drawing pins • Ribbon Sticky tape • Gaffa tape

Toy Hood by Piers Atkinson

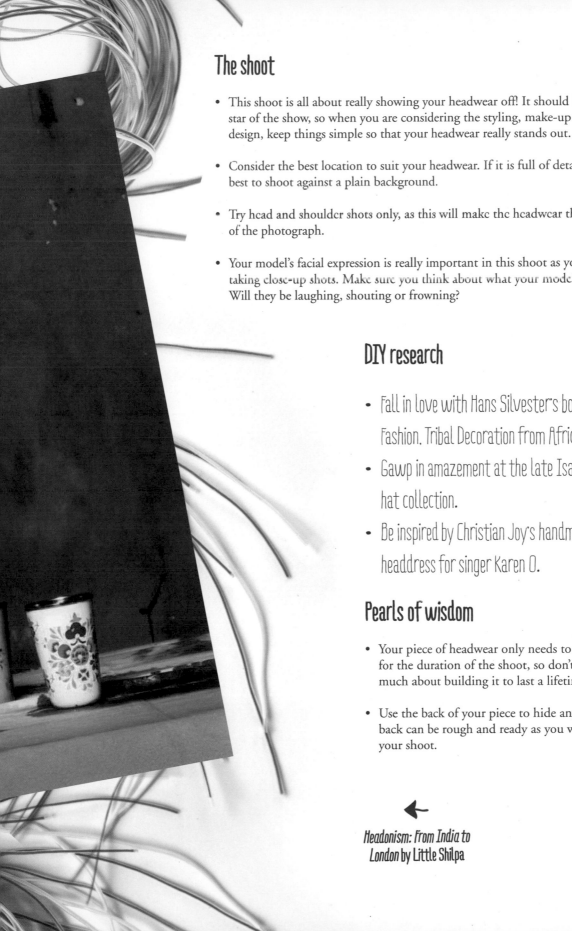

The shoot

- This shoot is all about really showing your headwear off! It should be the main star of the show, so when you are considering the styling, make-up and hair design, keep things simple so that your headwear really stands out.

- Consider the best location to suit your headwear. If it is full of detail, it might be best to shoot against a plain background.

- Try head and shoulder shots only, as this will make the headwear the main focus of the photograph.

- Your model's facial expression is really important in this shoot as you will be taking close-up shots. Make sure you think about what your model will be doing. Will they be laughing, shouting or frowning?

DIY research

- Fall in love with Hans Silvester's book 'Natural Fashion, Tribal Decoration from Africa'.
- Gawp in amazement at the late Isabella Blow's hat collection.
- Be inspired by Christian Joy's handmade headdress for singer Karen O.

Pearls of wisdom

- Your piece of headwear only needs to hold together for the duration of the shoot, so don't worry too much about building it to last a lifetime.

- Use the back of your piece to hide anything – the back can be rough and ready as you won't see this in your shoot.

Headonism: From India to London by Little Shilpa

A House of Fashion

Drafting in some SUPER-SIZED fashion props gives any shoot a BIG boost. Go cartoon, think XXL and blow run-of-the-mill objects up into super-sized caricatures of themselves. A huge rowing boat, giant geometric kites, oversized clocks, enormous clouds, massive lightning bolts. If you can't handle the idea of building 3D, relax, 2D objects can look just as exciting. Think GIANT, and don't stop making until every inch of your home is bursting with avant-garde constructions...

Step by step

1 You can design and build anything from a towering cupcake to a collection of collosal telephones. If you're feeling overwhelmed as to where to start, write down the alphabet in a list and then fill in as many objects as you can for each letter.

e.g **A** aeroplane, arrow, abacus, **B** butterfly, biscuit, bomb, **C** carrot, confetti, computer

2 Go through your list, and pick out your favourite(s).

3 Start sketching out your ideas. You might make one huge object like a hot air balloon, or a collection of objects that have a theme tying them together e.g. anchors and shells. THINK SUPERSIZE AT ALL TIMES!

4 Working from your drawings, brainstorm how the rest of the shoot will develop and go with it. Think about:

Art direction. Where would you find the super-sized objects you have chosen to make? Will you shoot them in their natural surroundings, or transport them into unusual surroundings.

Model(s). What sort of character(s) might you find hanging out with your chosen super-sized objects? How will they interact with each other?

Styling and make-up. How will these elements match the theme and colour scheme of your super-sized props?

5 Next, get building. You can make your props 3-D or 2-D, or a mixture of the two. Don't overthink how to make your objects, just grab materials and try things out. It can help to start with a basic structure like a large cardboard box, and then adapt it.

6 Try using different ways of fixing things together – glue can soak through card and paper so try double-sided sellotape or sticky tabs instead.

7 As you experiment with making, you may find that your objects change slightly. Don't worry too much if what you are building doesn't look exactly like your drawing, just go with whatever looks best in the flesh. The camera is very forgiving and the whole point of this shoot is to emulate a home-made, DIY style!

8 Prepare the rest of your shoot. Dress your model(s) and get going with their make-up and hair.

Helpful items

- Building materials (paper, cardboard, plastic, foam)
- Cardboard boxes (ask at your supermarket for old packing)
- Scissors/craft knife • Sellotape, double-sided sellotape • Blu-tack, glue, sticky pads •
- A stapler • Coloured pencils, paint, marker pens or felt tips

Daydreaming by Rebecca Miller

Untitled by William Selden

The shoot

- Make the most of your super-sized props. Focus on your art directing and try out different positions for your props, taking as much time as you need to arrange your models and props on set before picking up the camera.

- Make your model(s) to interact with the props – get them to have a laugh and try out different ways of working with the props.

DIY research

- Watch giant cardboard props come to life in short film *Bad Things That Could Happen* by This Is It
- Re-inspired by *The Magic Machine* by artists Jiggery Pokery and Jamie Brown
- Fall in love with Alexis Facca's paper art at paperdonut.com

Pearls of wisdom

- Move around when you are shooting! Move positions to capture each scene from all different angles.

- Your super-sized props don't need to be built to last forever, they only need to survive long enough to be photographed.

Dream a Little Dream of Me

From this very moment on, your only responsibility is to begin daydreaming. Forget about the humdrum of everyday life and allow your thoughts to drift far away, to wistful places and fanciful scenarios. Now you are galloping on a unicorn through storm clouds about to reach the outskirts of a gothic city or perhaps instead floating in a freshwater lake under a blanket of thick stars…

Wherever your mind elopes to, let it to go there. This is the only place you need to be to get into the right headspace for this next shoot.

Take a look at Ata Kandó's *Calypso & Nausicaa, South Italy (1956)*, shown here. It's beautiful. The sunset lighting, the Grecian styling, the ancient earthenware pots and the home-made headpiece all lull you into the image. You can almost hear the waves lapping in the background, as you stumble upon this mythical girl washed ashore from a bygone time…

'Stars shining bright above you
Night breezes seem to whisper "I love you"
Birds singing in the sycamore tree
Dream a little dream of me.'

Lyrics by Gus Kahn

Calypso & Nausicaa, South Italy (1956) by Ata Kandó

Helpful items

- An uncontrollable imagination

Step by step

1 If you haven't started daydreaming yet, do so now. Lie down, shut your eyes, breathe deeply and let your mind wander. After your daydreaming session, scribble down all the poetic ideas that have danced through your mind.

2 Look at your notes and think about which daydream you could transform into a shoot. The best way to pick one is to think about what you would need for each dream to become a reality. Work out which locations would be possible to find and what props you would need to get hold of to help narrow down your options.

3 Having trouble thinking of locations? Fantastical locations can be found in everyday settings close to your home so think about places that could create the right kind of atmosphere. Your shoot could take place at a river, a forest, a graveyard or even a local park. Alternatively, you could set dress somewhere at home. Drape coloured sheets from the ceilings in your bedroom, or string lace curtains from a tree in your garden.

4 The time of day that you choose to shoot at is really important. The mood at different times of the day changes with the sunlight, and this will determine the feeling of your photographs. Do you want your pictures to be filled with the eerie fog of early morning mists or the enchanting haze of late-summer evenings?

Pearls of wisdom

- Whichever location you use for your shoot make sure it is safe to go there and that you have permission if it is needed. Always go in a group or take someone older with you if you are wandering far from home.

- Make sure you allow yourself enough daylight hours. Let's say you are shooting at sunset — make sure you are at your location ready to go well before the sun goes down. This will give you time to set up and test your shots before the sun starts fading.

CHINA, Inner Mongolia. Horse Training for the Militia, 1979, by Eve Arnold

DIY research

- Listen to 'Love Me Tender' by Elvis Presley
- Fall in love with paintings by the Pre-Raphaelites
- Watch the 1999 film *Sleepy Hollow*

5 How will you style your models? Think about layering garments; long flowing dresses and silk veils. The styling should be as unusual as the daydream itself. If there isn't anything in your wardrobe, improvise. Fashion a dress by wrapping fabric around the body, tied at the waist with rope.

6 And what about hair and make-up? Go romantic with long, flowing locks and pastel make-up. Go gothic with pale faces and dark smoky eyes.

7 What is your model(s) mood in the photographs? Are they melancholy, vacant or dreamy? Are they motionless or are they skipping, spinning or lying down?

8 Beg, borrow or bargain-hunt some decent props. Fishing nets for catching butterflies (or souls), bags of feathers to throw in the air or flower petals to scatter on the ground.

The shoot

- Wondering how to capture the ultimate dreamy feel in your photos? Blow on your lens 'til the whole lens is covered in a 'fog'. Quickly shoot as the fog is disappearing and you'll find that your photograph has hazy edges and a dreamy feel. Keep experimenting, every result is different. Try out your own version of this technique by playing around with materials. Shoot through lace, coloured tights or anything else you can find that is almost transparent.

- Keep a real focus on the art directing! Capturing a mood and atmosphere is the most important thing for this shoot, so be hyper-aware of what pose and facial expression your model(s) have in each shot.

- Be inventive with your composition and framing. If you are shooting outside on a stormy day, shoot wide so that your model is surrounded by a dark, ominous sky or if your model is lying in the grass, shoot through the blades to create an interesting foreground.

CHEAP AS CHIPS

Head to any flea market or discount store and you'll be dazzled by treasures that stretch into the distance as far as your eye can see. Sift your way through old guitars, giant silk flowers, kitsch plastic pink flamingos and ornate, gold picture frames – most importantly, all with rock-bottom price tags. Shop 'til you drop, and buy wisely because you'll be basing a fashion shoot solely around your new purchases. Find and gather only the sublime, the ridiculous and the wonderful.

Helpful items
- A mode of transportation – all-important for ferrying home armfuls of bargains

A Million Miles by Susannah Benjamin Susannah shot this when she was 1 The use of the maps is a beautiful example of the multiple rule* at w

Step by step

1 Once you have located your nearest car boot sale or pound shop set yourself a shopping budget and stick to it. On a professional shoot it would be a big no-no to go over budget, so see this as good practice for spending within your means. Your budget doesn't need to be more than a few pounds, especially if you are heading to a car boot sale as things are superbly cheap.

2 On arrival, scour high and low, root around for the ideal props to base a fashion shoot around. Go for objects that you can't possibly leave behind or that could be made into something really unusual with a little work. Take your time and think through how you might use each item in a shoot.

3 Now you have your objects, what are you going to do with them? Dash home and let them be your guiding inspiration. What theme will you create from them? You could have a model in the shoot or try something different and make an unorthodox still life with them.

4 If it helps, set your objects out in front of you as you brainstorm your ideas. Most importantly, play around with your objects, experimenting with different ideas and possibilities.

5 Once you have hit upon your idea, consider all elements of the shoot. Think about the location, the art direction and if you are building a still life work out how you will arrange it. If you are using a model, work on the styling, the make-up and the hair design.

6 Storyboard out your shots and get ready for the shoot!

DIY research

Look in your local newspaper or search online to find your nearest car boot/bric-a-brac sale. Alternatively, find the location of your nearest discount store.

The shoot

- The driving force behind this shoot is the props, so do them justice. Experiment with your composition and framing, giving them the opportunity to really draw in the viewer's eye.

- Try positioning your props at different distances from the camera. Plan shots where they fill the foreground or others where they exist quietly in the background.

- As well as placing your props thoughtfully in the frame, get your model(s) to pick them up, sit on them, look through them or throw them in the air.

Pearls of wisdom

- If you are going to a flea market, arrive early to grab the best stuff.

- Haggle at flea markets. If you think the price of something is too high, offer less. People often agree as they just want to get rid of their unwanted stuff!

- When you are shopping, remember the multiples rule*: multiples of something can really make an image striking, so if you see hundreds of the same item for sale, snap them up.

THE STYLE SCOUT'S TREASURE HUNT

Three women standing on sidewalk, portrait by Emmanuel Faure

Style scouting is exactly what it says it is. It's hunting for style. It's looking for it everywhere and anywhere and it's finding it in people who have (often unknowingly) got it. With our Style Scout's Treasure Hunt you will perfect your skills at identifying real style – from classic chic to way-out-there fashion. It's time to celebrate the wonderfully different ways in which people dress, capturing it all with your camera!

Shooting style is an inspiring and delightful way to spend a day and what's great is that you can do it absolutely anywhere – on a holiday abroad or down at your local shopping centre. Whether you live in a tiny remote village or a bustling city, style can be found hiding in traditional work attire or in passing trends … all you've got to do is find it!

Helpful items
- Any kind of camera – from a camera phone to an SLR • A sharp eye and quick reflexes

DIY research
- Be inspired by The Sartorialist's blog
- Watch Bill Cunningham's *New York* the documentary about the daddy of style scouting.
- Gawp in amazement at *www.lookbook.nu* with its thousands of looks from around the globe.

Get started

Read the tips, grab a camera, tear out the treasure hunt list and head out! The only two things you need for style scouting are a camera and lots of people. Good luck!

Tips to Shooting in Public
Choose which approach is the one for you…

Approach No. 1
For the Bold. Approach the person and explain to them that you are style scouting. Tell them you think they look great and ask them politely if they would mind having their photograph taken.

Approach No. 2
For the Bashful. Snap the person without stopping them. At first you may feel like you keep missing people but after a bit of practice you'll be pleased to see how rapidly your technique improves.

Anna Dello Russo attending the Max Mara fashion show in Milan, Italy

The We Are Photogirls Style Scouting Treasure Hunt List

Tear out this page, then tick off on the list below once you have found and shot the following:

- ◯ Something BRIGHT
- ◯ Matching accessories
- ◯ Spots, stripes and patterns
- ◯ An unusual hairstyle
- ◯ Smart shoes
- ◯ Spring/summer/autumn/winter
  (depending on what time of year it is!)
- ◯ We heart moustaches
- ◯ Vintage fashion
- ◯ Most stylish business man/woman
- ◯ Your favourite lipstick shade
- ◯ Classic jewellery
- ◯ Colour clash
- ◯ Hippy dippy
- ◯ A hat to remember
- ◯ Fashionista pets
- ◯ Odd luggage
- ◯ Wacky watches
- ◯ Painted nails rule
- ◯ Double denim
- ◯ Big bows
- ◯ A dainty lady
- ◯ Twinkle twinkle little star
- ◯ Bold tattoos!
- ◯ RED is the colour of love
- ◯ Floral prints
- ◯ Eccentric style
- ◯ Unusual eyewear

I HAVE THE COOLEST BEDROOM

Whether your bedroom is big and spacious, tiny and cosy, bursting with clutter or neatly minimal, the day has come to transform it into the coolest bedroom imaginable. Forget what you see on predictable home makeover programmes. We're not talking about giving it a new lease of life by popping up some 'exciting' new curtains or adding a fresh lick of paint to the walls. This is bedroom design in the name of FASHION. See your bedroom as a blank canvas between four walls and convert it into a fashion set fit for any underground style magazine.

DIY research
- Be inspired by artist Sandy Skoglund's bedroom installations
- Gawp in amazement at artist Luise Valdes's Cardboard House

Untitled, 2004
by Katharina Grosse

Step by step
Put your thinking cap on.

1 Think bold, simple and effective. What could you do to really transform your bedroom? It could be as uncomplicated as turning your 'messy' bedroom into a tongue-in-cheek installation of millions of clothes strewn EVERYWHERE – on the floor, the walls and the ceiling. Or perhaps you, or someone you know, is a real collector? Suddenly your uncle's creepy taxidermy collection could become particularly interesting as you imagine stuffed animals perched on every surface in your bedroom. Go for a strong theme and make sure everything you do to your room suits it.

DO NOT DISTURB

(FASHION IN PROGRESS)

2 Moodboard your ideas and think through how you could practically make them happen. If you're planning to hang or attach objects in your room, work out how to do this without anything damaging your walls and ceilings! This could be as simple as pushing drawing pins in the ceiling to hang stuff from or by using fishing wire to suspend your objects.

3 Gather or make what you need for your transformation. You may have to be really inventive in sourcing or making the items you need, so call in favours from friends and consider borrowing items too.

4 Stand in your bedroom and assess what furniture needs to go and what can stay, leaving only what your new bedroom needs. When you have done this, move the remaining items and objects around until you are completely happy with the set-up.

5 Now it's time to dress your bedroom. Have your camera with you so that you can look through the viewfinder to see how things are shaping up along the way.

6 Get shooting! Try photographing your new room from different viewpoints. You could even go one step further and style yourself to suit your new bedroom and get a friend to shoot a portrait of you in it!

Pearls of wisdom

- If you are planning to do something radical like painting a mural from floor to ceiling it won't be so easy to change back, so make sure you can handle living with the consequences!
- Remember that a simple idea can be just as effective as a complicated one.
- Really go for it. Take your concept to the extreme!

FASHION FAMILY PORTRAITURE

You have probably seen quite a few family portraits hanging up in the homes of your friends and relatives over the years. The people in them change from home to home but there's something very similar about all of them. They are filled with shiny happy families dressed in smart outfits with angelic smiles that beam at us through the camera lens.

They are pleasant enough pictures to have around, but why not make one with a little more character and flair? One that says a little bit more about your family and that will have a real impact on future generations as they walk past it hanging in the hallway!

Let your family be your canvas, go as crazy on them as they will allow you to!

DIY research

- Be inspired by the styling in the 1960s TV series 'The Addams Family'
- Listen to Sister Sledge's corny anthem 'We Are Family'
- Gawp in amazement at www.awkwardfamilyphotos.com

Helpful items
- As many family members as you can find lying around the house

Dutch family from
w.awkwardfamilyphotos.com

Shot by Matt Irwin
For *Dazed & Confused*

Brighton Rabbits
by Charlotte Cory

HENNAH & KENT.   BRIGHTON

Step by step

1 Start off by brainstorming ideas for your fashion family portrait. There are countless ways in which to reinvent, restyle and record your family.

Think about:
Using a family hobby to theme the shoot around.
Giving your family a unified look e.g. they could all be dressed in the same outfit.
Styling them with matching over-the-top hairdos.
Picking a tongue-in-cheek theme or era to dress them up in.
Bringing your pets onboard to feature in the shoot.

2 Creating personas for your family members is a must! In the Dutch family portrait notice how the facial expressions and props really add character to the photograph. Make sure each person in your shoot knows exactly how you would like them to stand, sit and pose. When storyboarding your ideas, note down different facial expressions and compositions.

3 Where are you going to shoot your family portrait? Traditionally, a family portrait would be taken in a photography studio in front of a backdrop. You could follow convention by choosing a fabric or wallpaper that you like, hanging it up and shooting your family in front of it. The other options are to photograph your family somewhere in your home, or to look outdoors for a location. The background of your portrait is very important, so take your time to think about what really suits your theme.

4 Gather together the outfits you will need for each family member. Whether you have chosen a group styling theme or individual looks, make sure you have a clear vision in mind and stick to it. You might be able to get your family to help

you find items. Are there bits and pieces that you need to source, borrow or make? Don't forget to look around your house for props that could add that something extra to your shoot.

5 Get the whole family to put a date in the diary for your shoot. Find a time when everyone has an evening or a day free so that there is no rush and everyone can relax and enjoy the experience.

6 Once you have got everyone dressed and ready to go, grab your storyboard. Organizing a group into different compositions is tricky, so make sure you follow your drawings to help you stay in control. Now you are ready to start shooting.

P.S If you want to be in your family portrait you could ask a friend to be the photographer. Or, if your camera has a self-timer use it, and jump in the frame at the last moment.

Pearls of wisdom

- If you can't get the whole family to be in your shoot don't worry. It can feature as few or as many people as you can get hold of (e.g. if you can persuade your gran to let you style her within an inch of her life!).

- If you are stuck for ideas, get your family involved in the brainstorming.

- If you have a lot of people in your shoot, you will need to arrange them very neatly to squeeze them all into your frame! Try standing taller people at the back and sit smaller people down at the front. In your DIY research keep an eye out for compositions that you like and could mimic in your shoot.

SWAPARAMA

One man's junk is another man's treasure. Or so the saying goes. If you're low on cash but desperate for 'that special something' to breath new life into your fashion shoots, it's time for Swaparama.

A Swaparama is an event where you and your friends trade make-up, jewellery, hair accessories, props, backdrops, clothes and shoes. But this is no ordinary swap. Anything that would be described as 'everyday' or 'normal' can forget it. ONLY items fit for a shoot get to join in – they need to be outrageous, beautiful, the right side of wrong, exotic and must have something special about them…

The Swaparama will come to a head in an auction frenzy with you acting as 'auctioneer' and your guests bidding wildly on must-have items. Keep your Swaparama intimate by inviting a few friends and hosting in your living room or go extravagant and hire a hall, invite everyone and tell the press….

Invite

You need guests! To get started, use your home as a venue, set a date and get your invites out. Give your guests enough time to have a good rummage for items. On the day, all they need to do is turn up with their swap items in tow. Oh, and be sure to tell them this Swaparama is for exceptional, shoot-worthy items *ONLY*!!!!

Hunt

Ransack your wardrobe, climb through your attic, root through every cupboard in your house, empty your jewellery box on the floor. Hunt high and low for anything you own that you have grown tired of. Make-up, jewellery, hair accessories, props, backdrops, clothes, shoes, even camera equipment…

Two models on a cruise, sponsored by *Picture Post*, choose their outfits for the day, 1955

Host

This part is boring but it has to be done…you need to set up two areas 'the goods area' and 'the auction area.' Clear your hosting room as much as possible to give you space.

Your 'auction area' needs to consist of somewhere for your guests to sit, a clear space for you to stand, and an area next to you to display all the items on offer. Guests could sit on sofas, chairs, beanbags or on the floor, while you, the 'auctioneer' will stand in front of them.

Next, set up the 'goods area'. Make some signs for 'MAKE-UP', 'ACCESSORIES', 'CLOTHES', 'SHOES', 'PROPS', and 'MISCELLANEOUS' and designate different areas in your room for the different categories . Use any surface – the floor, the table, shelves, etc.

Get hold of tokens that you will give to guests in exchange for their items. You could use poker chips or raffle tickets or make your own tokens.

As each person arrives, get them to add their items to the correct areas. Don't forget to add yours too.

> Give each person tokens for their items. Follow this system:
>
> **10 tokens** – items that are quite good
>
> **20 tokens** – items that are great
>
> **25 tokens** – items that are exceptionally brilliant
>
> **30 tokens** – items that are out of this world

When all your guests have arrived and all the wonderful Swaparama items have been exchanged for tokens, it's time for a little window shopping. Get everyone to take a good look at everything on offer and decide what is of interest, because in a minute it's going to get crazy…

As you are the auctioneer, ask a friend to bid on the items you want. Decide how many tokens you are willing to use to get what you want so that they know what your limit is.

The auction

- You need a hammer and a very loud voice.

- Go through each item. Hold it up, describe it with full auctioneer flair, and set a low price (e.g. 2 tokens) to get things going. Or you could ask a friend to act as 'co-auctioneer' to help you, holding up the items and describing them as you take care of the bidding. Then the bidding begins!

- The item goes to whoever bids the highest amount. Repeat this process until everything in the auction has been offered. Any unwanted goods can go back to the original owner and unwanted tokens can be taken back.

- The auction draws to a close and everyone can enjoy their new prized possessions! N.B. Absolutely no punching, kicking, biting, scratching or hair pulling allowed! All's fair in love and Swaparama…

Mixte editorial 2 image/hair
by Sandra Freij

And Finally

HOW TO EDIT YOUR PHOTOGRAPHS TO PERFECTION

Once the final shot has been taken and the last of the props packed away, you may think that the fashion shoot is drawing to an end. But there's one final stage that hasn't even begun yet and that is…

Editing

Editing photographs is a skill unto itself. A vital stage of every shoot, this is the moment of truth where you get to pore over each and every one of your shots. Understanding how to identify the strongest photographs takes time and concentration, but once you've got the hang of it, it'll just get easier and easier.

How do I edit?

It's easy to end up with a billion and one photos from a shoot. So where do you even begin? Upload your photos onto a computer and open them in whichever photo package you have. Next, start by making a 'rough edit'. Open a new folder and name it 'rough edit'. Now, go through your photographs taking the ones that you like and dropping them into this folder. Pick ones that you feel have something special about them, e.g. a great energy, strong atmosphere, beautiful lighting or an unusual composition. Be generous at this stage, remember it's only a 'rough' edit!

Now step away from the computer. Your eyes need time away from the images to see them clearly again. Come back in a few hours or the next day to re-edit further.

When you return, your next goal is to edit your selection of images further to make a group that work *together*. Flicking through any magazine fashion shoot, you'll notice that the photographs have been put together in an order that creates a visual 'story'. You too are creating a visual fashion story. Like any story, you'll need to have a beginning, middle and end; you'll need characters, little details and an overview, so pick photographs that communicate these elements. Start a 'final edit' folder and only drag in the shots from your 'rough edit' folder that are the strongest. Most importantly, keep double-checking that the ones you choose work together as a group. You may even decide to choose an image based on whether it does or doesn't complement the rest of the shots you have chosen. Aim to end up with 8-12 shots in your final edit.

When you are editing, here are some tips to help you identify which photographs to choose…

The composition

As well as going for conventional fashion compositions, look for shots that break the rules. Sometimes the more unusual images, including shots that were taken by accident (!), have a distinctiveness that make them stand out from the crowd.

The facial expressions

The model will have had various facial expressions during the shoot. Think about which expressions feel the most convincing and convey the appropriate feeling you want for your shoot. Do you want the work to have a happy, sad, contemplative or dreamy tone?

The body language

Notice your model's body language in the shots. You want the model's body to look comfortable and at home. Even if the intention was to strike some strange poses, you'll still notice the ones that look uncomfortable. You want your model to look 'natural', even when doing the most 'unnatural' things with her body.

The styling

Keep a beady eye out for tiny details in the styling. Don't let a visible stylist's clamp or label slip through your net into the final edit.

The lighting

The lighting can make or break a photograph. Make sure that the lighting in your photographs reflects the mood that you want. Sometimes odd or unusual lighting can look fantastic. A bleached-out photograph with parts of the image 'blown out' (this is where parts of the image disappears into white) can look dramatic if it suits the theme of the shoot.

P.S
When you are showing your work to people you want to impress, ONLY show your final edits! The greatest fashion photographers don't take amazing shots every single time, but they are very selective about what they show.

P.P.S
Shot the MOST amazing photograph, but it's just a bit too dark? There's nothing wrong with turning to the help of a photo-editing package. Free ones can be found on the internet or get a copy of Photoshop if you can afford it. Using a photo-editing package learn how to adjust the lighting, colours and contrast of your photographs.

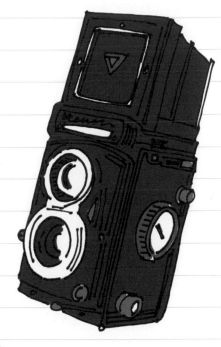

IT'S A NEW DAWN, IT'S A NEW DAY...

After rising to the many challenges you have come across in this book you will not only have an amazing portfolio of photographs that you have worked on, but also have an insider's knowledge of exactly how a fashion shoot works.

Whether you decide that you'd like to keep making fashion shoots as a passionate hobby, or whether you'd like to take it further as a career, here's some advice that we thought might be helpful.

It's time to...

1 **Share your work** with your fellow Photogirls by posting your shoots on our Facebook page.

2 **Get a blog!** Blogs are fantastic because they are free, really easy to use and allow you to showcase your work to the whole wide world. They also broaden your knowledge of your contemporaries, by allowing you to join communities of other bloggers whose work will excite and inspire you. There are several blogging websites you can use – Wordpress and Blogger are two of the most popular. For a real visual treat try out Tumblr, where you can create a purely image-based blog.

3 **Get an online portfolio.** This is soooooooooo easy. Just go to sites like Flickr and Instagram, create an account, and start uploading your photographs. You can also join groups of other photographers who have similar interests to you, as well as receiving feedback on your pictures from like-minded souls.

4 **Never give up!** Keep making fashion shoots happen! Whether you are obsessed with styling or adore make-up design, team up with friends and organize shoots whenever you have the time. Keep scrapbooks and make moodboards for shoots that you want to create in the future.

Next steps

Many successful creative people have made a name for themselves by starting out down the DIY route. This means get out there. Use your creativity and imagination and think up inventive ways to make things happen for yourself.

Doing something is ALWAYS better than doing nothing. Here are some thoughts for you to run with…

• Start your own online magazine

• Organize a one-night-only exhibition of your and your friends' photographs

• Form a collective and meet regularly to discuss ideas of what you are going to do – for example, get a market stall and sell your photographs or hand-made gems.

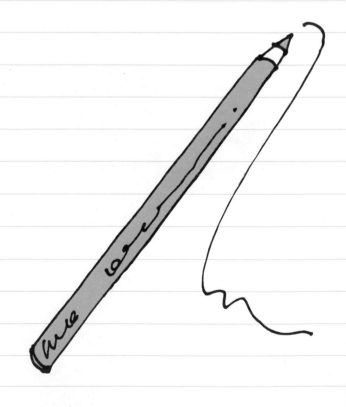

A GUIDE TO GETTING THROUGH WORK EXPERIENCE

Work experience is a good way to get a real feel for whether or not you like the reality of working in the industry. Getting hold of a placement and making the most of it when you do can feel tricky. Our tips below will help you out.

How to get great work experience

One good place to start is to ask older relatives and their friends if they have any contacts. Another is to check out magazine shoots and find ones that you like. Search the internet for the people who worked on them and get in touch via their website's contact page. Who you should approach depends on what area you are particularly interested in – don't waste your time doing work experience with a hair stylist if you actually want to be a photographer.

Write an introductory email. Keep it brief, don't ramble on and lose their interest. Write a brief paragraph *only*, being really enthusiastic about what they do as well as what you want to do. Tell them you are happy to make cups of tea, and you just want to get your foot in the door. Send a link to your blog or online portfolio, or attach an example of your work.

N.B. If you are attaching files of your work, ALWAYS make sure that the files are small. There's nothing more awkward than jamming up the inbox of someone you are trying to impress!

Chase up your emails. Don't ever feel disheartened if you don't get an immediate response. If you don't hear back in a week, follow up with a polite email or be brave and call them up. They will be impressed by your enthusiasm and dedication! Don't give up hope after the first attempt, keep trying, and trying, and trying, and trying…

If you don't hear back at all, don't take it personally. Ninety-nine per cent of the time if people don't reply to emails it's just because they are too damn busy. Approach several people/places to guarantee a higher chance of success.

And when (not if!) you get that coveted placement, here are some tips for how to impress. Because if you do, you could be offered a job at the end of it.

- Never ever be late! Be bang on time, everyday.

- Dress well. This doesn't mean you have to wear a power suit but first impressions count so no matter what your style, make sure you are well turned out.

- Never ever use your phone on the job. It'll look like you've got better things to do. The same goes for having a cheeky look on Facebook or checking your emails. Others might do it, but you're there on your best behaviour, so don't.

- Be super helpful. Offer to do things. Use your own initiative and do simple, obvious things that look like they need to be done – like offering to take a visitor's coat when they arrive at an office. Stay late if needed and do your best to show that there's no job too big or small that you aren't willing to take on.

- You might luck out and get a really exciting work experience placement, or… you might not! Even if you are bored stupid, keep a smile on and stay ready and eager. At least you can then leave with your head held high, safe in the knowledge that if anyone ever gets in touch to ask how you were, they'll have to say you were brilliant.

- Don't gossip or moan. Even if you end up working for a complete monster don't badmouth them to other people working there. Save that treat for your friends!

Picture Credits

We Are Photogirls would like to say a HUGE thank you to all the artists who have allowed us to feature their incredible work in this book!

Laurence King Publishing would like to thank the individuals and institutions who have kindly provided photographic material for use in this book. While every effort has been made to trace the present copyright holders we apologise in advance for any unintentional omission or error and will be pleased to insert the appropriate acknowledgement in any subsequent edition.

p.3 *Circus!* By Lucy Kenny. Model Tallulah Haddon. Photography by Lucy Kenny, 16 years old.

pp.8–9 and p.71 *Girls on Bikes* by Elaine Constantine. Photographer: Elaine Constantine. Stylist: Polly Banks. Agent: Santucci & Co www.santucciandco.com

p.17 *Wonderland – Afternoon Nap* by Yeondoo Jung 2004, 100 x 125 cm

p.18 Louise Dahl-Wolfe by Robert Doisneau / Getty Images

p.20-21 *Beachobatics* by George Caddy

p.24 *Untitled* from the *Qajar* series, 1998 by Shadi Ghadirian

p.25 *Kim, 15, Tampa, Florida* by Danielle Levitt

p.28 *Bridget* by Olaf Breuning

p.30 (left) A model presents a creation designed by John Galliano, 20 January 2003 in Paris for Christian Dior Spring / Summer 2003 Haute Couture collection / Getty Images (right) A model on the runway at the Christian Dior Spring/Summer 2008 collection fashion show/ © Stephane Cardinale / People Avenue / Corbis

p.33 An image from *Quant on Make-up*, photograph by Robyn Beeche (1986). Make-up and design by Phyllis Cohen for Mary Quant

p.35 *Queen Marie Antoinette* by Jean-Etienne Liotard (1702–89) / Hofburg, Vienna, Austria / The Bridgeman Art Library

p.38 Audrey Hepburn as Holly Golightly. Film title: *Breakfast At Tiffany's* directed by Blake Edwards; film company: Paramount; 05 October 1961 © AF archive / Alamy

p.40 *Roses Are Red But My Sweater Is Pink* by Sunshine Tucker. Created solely by Sunshine Tucker

p.43 Cover of the Ronettes' single, *Walking in the Rain* / Michael Ochs Archives / Getty Images

p.45 Members of the Jimi Hendrix Experience doing their hair, c.1968. Popperfoto / Getty Images

p.49 *Frida on White Bench* by Nickolas Muray © Nickolas Muray Photo Archives

p.50 Swimsuit Girls of Old Japan Rob Oechsle Collection http://www.flickr.com/photos/24443965@N08/2336103245/

p.52 AW11 lookbook image by Fred Butler Styled by Kim Howells, directed by Elisha Smith Leverock. Bracelet and ball by Fred Butler

p.54 Jordan c.1970 by Caroline Greville-Morris /Redferns

p.55 *Punk Girls in Hyde Park, 1985* by Gavin Watson

p.59 *Inside the Cloud* by Zim&Zou Art direction – Zim&Zou / Chris Christiano (*Wired Magazine*)

p.61 *Construct* by Agnes Lloyd-Platt

p.63 *Jump For My Love* by Ichbinkong Artist: Timm Schneider aka Kong. Helping hands: Tri-An Huynh, Wibke Scharpenberg, Matthias Zosel, Martin Weiss

p.65 *The Obliteration Room* by Yayoi Kusama, Installation at the Gallery of Modern Art, Brisbane Courtesy: Ota Fine Arts, Tokyo / © Yayoi Kusama / Photograph: Natasha Harth, QAGOMA

p.68 *Hotel* by Cari Ann Wayman *Two Guns* by Cari Ann Wayman

pp.74–75 Images by Lisa Comeford, Elle Benton at Yellow Bird Photography and Tita Beaufrand

pp.76–77 *Teenagers Dancing and Listening to Rock 'n' Roll on the Beach* by Lynn Pelham

p.84 *Pomworld* by Beinta á Torkilsheyggi Photo by Beinta á Torkilsheyggi, pom poms by Pom Pom Factory

p.87 *To Do* by Illegal Art www.illegalart.org

p.89 *mixte editorial 2 image/stage* by Sandra Freij. Photographer: Sandra Freij; stylist: Sarah Cobb; hair: Tracy Cahoon

p.91 *Picnic Dress Tent* by Robin Lasser and Adrienne Pao. H 122cm x W102cm Chromogenic print, 2005. Dress Tents www.robinlasser.com www.adriennepao.com www.dresstents.com

p.93 *Cleaner | pugh-atory | 2010* by Madame Peripetie Photographer / art director / sculpture: Madame Peripetie. Photo assistant: blackshift. Model: Xenia

p.95 *Fairy Bread* by The Girls (Andrea Blood and Zoe Sinclair). Date of work: 2007 www.thegirls.co.uk

p.97 *Girl at the Listening Vessel* by Diana Hooper Bloomfield © Diana Hooper Bloomfield

p.99 *Lola* by Sarah Roesink, 2004, pinhole photograph on photographic colour paper

p.101 Splash Calendar 2011 – 'War' by Tejal Patni Photography/ concept – Tejal Patni; wardrobe stylist Kirsten Hermans; production design – Andrew del Rosario; model – Sofi Longhurst; hair and make-up – Sofi Longhurst; digital retouching – Anil Palyekar; illustrator – Lia Golemba

p.103 Still from Robert Siodmak's film *The Spiral Staircase* starring Dorothy McGuire © Moviestore collection Ltd / Alamy

p.104 *Untitled* by William Selden *Vogue Hommes Japan*. Styling: Nicola Formichetti; hair and make-up Kamo; jacket: Top Man

p.105 *Toy Hood* by Piers Atkinson

pp.106–07 *Headonism: from India to London* by Little Shilpa. Headpiece and styling: Shilpa Chavan; photography: Prasad Naik; model: Suchitra Pillai

p.109 *Daydreaming* by Rebecca Miller Photograph taken by Rebecca Miller for Image Source. Copyright both Rebecca Miller and Image Source

p.110 *Untitled* by William Selden *Another Man*. Styling: Nicola Formichetti; all clothes: Paul Smith; hair: Tomo Jidai; make-up: Ayami Nishimura; set design and model: Gary Card

pp.112–13 *Calypso and Nausicaa, South Italy (1956)* by Ata Kandó

p.115 *CHINA, Inner Mongolia. Horse training for the militia. 1979* by Eve Arnold © Eve Arnold / Magnum Photos

pp.116–17 *A Million Miles* by Susannah Benjamin

p.119 Three women standing on sidewalk, portrait by Emmanuel Faure / Getty Images

p.120 Anna Della Russo attending the Max Mara fashion show on February 23, 2012 in Milan, Italy / Getty Images

p.121 *Chihuahua Mexico* by Tita Beaufrand. Tita Beaufrand, graphic designer and photographer, Caracas, Venezuela

p.123 *Untitled*, 2004 by Katharina Grosse acrylic on wall, floor and various objects, approx 280 x 450 x 400cm. Foto Nic Tenwiggenhorn. © Katharina Grosse und VG Bild-Kunst Bonn, 2013

p.127 (bottom left) Dutch Family / awkwardfamilyphotos.com (top right) Shot by Matt Irwin for *Dazed & Confused*

p.128 *Brighton Rabbits* by Charlotte Cory / The Green Parrots Gallery, Greenwich

p.130 Two of the models on a cruise, sponsored by *Picture Post,* choose their outfits for the day ahead. Original Publication: *Picture Post* – 7850 – Five Girls On A Yacht – pub.1955 Getty Images

p.134–35 *mixte editorial 2 image/hair* by Sandra Freij. Photographer: Sandra Freij; stylist: Sarah Cobb; hair: Tracy Cahoon

Front cover: left, William Selden; right Susannah Benjamin. Back cover: © 2009 Manuel Miniño. Cover flap: Cari Ann Wayman.

Who are We Are Photogirls?

We Are Photogirls was started by two friends, Emily and Celia who met at art college in the 1990s. We Are Photogirls is a London-based organization that specializes in engaging girls through the media of fashion, style and photography, through events, projects and fashion shoot parties. We Are Photogirls also consults and art directs for those looking to engage the teenage mind.

After seven years of running fashion photography projects and events for trillions of young enthusiasts, we have put together a mixture of our most loved and adored fashion shoot challenges for you to try, as well as brand-new and unseen ones too. So wherever you are in the world you can now join in from the comfort of your own home. We hope you enjoy the book and that one day we will get to meet you.

Showcasing your work, meeting other photogirls and staying inspired

First thing's first, befriend us on Facebook. We'd love to see your shoots, so when you finish one from the book, share it with us by posting your favourites from it on our wall. Here you can also meet other Photogirls and check out what they have been up to. For an emporium of never-ending fashion shoot inspiration, follow our We Are Photogirls Tumblr blog. And if you ever need any advice, just drop us a line.

Goodbye for now and good luck! We can't wait to see what you do.

If you ever have any questions we are here to help. so get in touch:

www.wearephotogirls.com

http://www.wearephotogirls.tumblr.com

Search for We Are Photogirls on Facebook.

**we are\\\\\
PHOTOGIRLS**

→

Use the handy pocket opposite for all your tearsheets and notes